BERLIN
Manfred Hamm

BERLIN

PHOTOGRAPHIEN VON MANFRED HAMM

Mit einem Essay von Klaus Hartung

deutsch · english

nicolai

Bei den Abbildungen auf den Seiten 10, 15, 18, 21 handelt es sich um sogenannte Schwarzpläne. Sie zeigen lediglich die existierenden Bauten und präsentieren damit die Textur der Stadt. In ihrer Abfolge, zu lesen von links oben nach rechts unten, dokumentieren sie die tiefgreifenden Veränderungen von vier zentralen Stadtarealen Berlins.

The pages 10, 15, 18, 21 show so-called "black plans". These display only the existing buildings and thereby present the texture of the city. As a series read from above left to below right they document the far-reaching changes undergone by four central areas of Berlin.

Berlin im Zeichen der Selbstbesinnung

von Klaus Hartung

I. Auf der Suche nach dem verlorenen Stadtbild

Grundmelodie. Das Neue, das diese Photographien zeigen, ist etwas, das immer schon da war. Sie machen sichtbar, was seit jeher vor Augen stand. Aber es bedurfte erst einer Archäologie der Evidenz, damit wir es sehen. Die Photographien von Manfred Hamm haben ihre eigene Sprache. Wir blättern und lesen und entdecken in ihnen die ästhetische Grammatik und die Parameter der Schönheit Berlins. Da klingt eine Grundmelodie auf: ernst, selbstbewußt, schwerblütig-heiter, klassisch-lakonisch – ein *andante assai maestoso.* Aus steinernen Zeugen, Spolien bürgerlichen Selbstbewußtseins, aufklärerischen Anstrengungen, industrieller Hochkultur und humanistischer Bildung organisiert Berlin seine Spannung zwischen Geschichte und Moderne. All das wird gezeigt. Es ist wahr und erscheint so selbstverständlich wie die Muttersprache. Und dennoch – nichts davon ist wirklich vertraut. Vor unseren Augen entfaltet sich vielmehr eine machtvolle Stadtvision, die wohl auch im Hintergrund des täglichen Augenscheins schlummert, aber seit langem nicht mehr wachgerufen wurde. Es ist eine Vision im strengen Sinne, also etwas, das erst er-sehen werden mußte.

Diese Vision spricht für sich selbst. Um sie zu sehen, bedarf es keiner weiteren Worte. Aber da Bücher nun einmal ihre Schicksale haben, ist es nicht ohne Bedeutung, wann und wo sie erscheinen. Das gilt ganz besonders für dieses Werk. Es ist eine Zeit tiefgreifenden Wandels in einem Ort, der sich selbst radikal verändert. Diese Photographien beteiligen sich an dem leidenschaftlichen Selbstgespräch, in das die Stadt sich verstrickt hat. Weil in Zeiten der Veränderung Mißverständnisse der Normalfall sind und weil Hamms Bildband in einem Berlin des Übergangs erscheint, muß auch über die *Position* dieses Werkes geredet werden. Daß hier keine realistische Berlinreportage vorliegt, ist offen-

Berlin within a framework of self-reflection

by Klaus Hartung

I. *In search of the lost city image*

Fundamental theme. *The New, as represented by these photographs, is something that has always been there. Things which have always existed are made visible by these images. However, this enhancement of our perception has only been made possible by an archaeology of the evidence. Manfred Hamm's photographs have their own language. As we turn the pages and read, we discover the aesthetic grammar and the parameters of Berlin's beauty. A fundamental melodic theme emerges: earnest, self-assured, ponderously cheerful, classically laconic – an* andante assai maestoso. *Berlin formulates its tension between history and modernity in terms of the testimony of stone, traces of bourgeois self-confidence, Enlightenment aspirations, the high culture of industrial society and humanist scholarship. All this is rendered perceptible. It is true and seems to be as natural as one's mother tongue. Yet, none of it is really familiar. Rather, what unfolds before our eyes is a powerful vision of the city, one that slumbers in the background of our everyday field of perception, but which has long remained obscure. It is a vision in the stricter sense, and as a result must first be truly perceived.*

This vision speaks for itself. The act of seeing does not require words. However, since books tend to have their own particular destinies, the question of when and where they are published is not without significance. This applies particularly to this work. It is a time of fundamental change in a place which is itself radically changing. These photographs participate in the city's intense discussion with itself. Since misunderstandings are perfectly normal in times of change, and since Hamm's book of photographs is being published in a Berlin which is in transition, the position *of this work also requires discussion. It is obvious that this book is by no means a realistic photographic documentation of the city. However, one must be wary of misunderstanding the aesthetic grammar of the city that these photographs reveal as*

sichtlich. Aber es muß wohl vor dem Mißverständnis gewarnt werden, die ästhetische Grammatik der Stadt, die diese Photographien sichtbar machen, würde nur eine Quersumme von schönen Ansichten und Sehenswürdigkeiten darstellen. Das Thema Schönheit der Stadt ist in diesem historischen Moment in Berlin brisant und weitaus mehr als nur eine Ansichtssache. Es geht um mehr als um das „nur Ästhetische". Denn in der widerspruchsvollen und rätselhaften Berliner Geschichte bahnt sich eine Wende an, und das Buch ist Teil dieser Wende.

Wende. Die Berliner haben mit der Lektüre ihrer Stadt begonnen und fangen an, ihre Sprache neu zu buchstabieren. Sie werden zu Touristen in ihrer eigenen Stadt, erforschen ihre geschichtliche Gestalt, entdecken ihre *points de vue* und Veduten wieder. Die Bildsprache Hamms ist geradezu ein Propädeutikum dieser Anstrengung. Unübersehbar ist ihr Gestus der Einladung. Der unausgesprochene Imperativ dieser Bildfolgen ruft: Folgt uns! Sie sind auch das Portal, das zu den *mystères de Berlin,* zum tieferen Verständnis der Stadt führt. Die Klassizität ihres Duktus ergibt sich keineswegs bruchlos; sie sind vielmehr der einzigartigen Paradoxie und Exzentrik dieser Stadt abgewonnen, die zu Recht die Stadtplaner, Architekten, Philosophen und Literaten überall in der Welt beschäftigt und anzieht. Was aber gezeigt wird, ist nicht einfach das, was Berlin ist; es ist vor allem das Gerettete, das, was trotz allem überlebte, was der Gegenwart standhielt – es ist die zu Herzen gehende Unzerstörbarkeit der Stadt. Es ist das Berliner Stadtbild.

Stadtbildlose Metropole. Das Berliner Stadtbild? Hinter diesen Begriff hat Berlin zunächst einmal ein großes Fragezeichen gesetzt. Was in anderen europäischen Städten immer auch der Stolz der *civitas* ist, nämlich das Stadtbild, scheint in Berlin bestenfalls eine Nebensache zu sein. Wer ein Berliner Stadtbild beschwört, wie Manfred Hamm es tut, der riskiert etwas, mindestens den Verdacht, zu harmonisieren und schönzufärben. Aber diese Photographien glätten nicht, sondern widersprechen dem herrschenden Konsens und Selbstbild Berlins. In diesem Buch, das so klassisch daherkommt, steckt Radikalität. Hier wird ein konsequentes Gegenparadigma formuliert. Denn Berlin war und ist nachgerade stolz, sich von der Hegemonie *eines* Stadtbildes befreit zu haben. Die vorherrschende Vorstellung von der Berliner Identität kreist um ganz andere Schlüsselbegriffe: Sie beschwören das Fragmentarische, das Inkohärente, das Heterogene, verbunden bestenfalls als Collage. Es herrscht der geheime Konsens einer stadtbildlosen Metropole.

Konglomerat. Dieses Selbstverständnis ist keineswegs leicht nachzuvollziehen. Es wirkt wie eine sehr intellektuelle und sehr exzentrische Außenseiterposition. Aber es ist weitverbreitet und eigentlich ganz alltäglich. Man hat sich in Ber-

representing an amalgamation of attractive views and interesting landmarks. At the present moment in Berlin's history, the theme of urban aesthetics is an explosive one and far more than merely a matter of opinion. At issue is more than "mere aesthetics." For Berlin, with its contradictory and baffling history is on the verge of change, and this book is part of that change.

Transition. *Berliners have started to read their city and are beginning to learn the new alphabet of its language. They are becoming tourists in their own city, are exploring its historical formation, and rediscovering its* points de vue *and vedute. Hamm's pictorial language is nothing short of a preparatory course for this endeavour. Its beckoning gesture is inescapable. The unarticulated imperative of this series of pictures calls out: Follow us! They are the portals that lead to the* mystères de Berlin, *to a deeper understanding of the city. Their classical character is by no means seamless. Rather, they take on the uniquely paradoxical nature and eccentricity of this city, which is understandably occupying and attracting town planners, architects, philosophers and writers throughout the world. But the book does not simply show what Berlin is; it focuses above all on what has been saved, what, in spite of everything, has survived, has resisted the impact of the present – it is the moving indestructability of the city. It is the Berlin city image.*

Metropolis without a city image. *The Berlin city image? In the first place, Berlin has placed a large question mark beside this concept. Whereas in other European cities, the city image is a source of pride for the inhabitants, in Berlin it seems to be at best secondary. Anyone who evokes a city image of Berlin, as Manfred Hamm does, runs the risk of at least being suspected of creating an artificial harmony and glossing over reality. However, rather than creating a unitary surface, these photographs contradict the prevailing consensus and self-image of Berlin. This book, which appears to adhere to the classical model, is in fact radical in its approach. It formulates a coherent counter-paradigm. For Berlin was and still is proud of having freed itself from the hegemony of a single city image. The dominant idea of Berlin's identity focuses on quite different key concepts. These refer to the fragmentary, the incoherent, the heterogeneous, interlinked at best as a collage. There is a dominant unspoken consensus that Berlin is a metropolis without a city image.*

Conglomeration. *This self-interpretation is by no means easy to comprehend. It conveys the impression of a highly intellectualised and extremely eccentric outsider stance. But it is widespread and quite commonplace. In Berlin, people have become accustomed to thinking that there is no need for such a thing as a classic city image. They live in a modern city where what counts is functionality, cheap rents and wide streets free of traffic congestion. Apart from this, most Berliners embrace the myth that the classic city image and the old Berlin disappeared together with the Third Reich. On the other hand, it is noticeable that*

lin angewöhnt, der Meinung zu sein, so etwas wie ein klassisches Stadtbild bräuchte man nicht. Man lebt in einer modernen Stadt, und da zählen Funktionalität, preiswerte Mieten und breite Straßen ohne Stau. Außerdem hängt der größte Teil der Berliner dem Mythos an, daß das klassische Stadtbild und das alte Berlin zusammen mit dem Dritten Reich untergegangen seien. Allerdings fällt auf, daß dieses Selbstverständnis sehr heftig verteidigt wird. Man spürt den angestrengten Anspruch einer Stadt, die von der Geschichte aus der Bahn geworfen wurde und sich dazu verdammt sieht, anders als andere Städte zu sein. Da ist auch Verzicht erkennbar, und der ziehende Schmerz über das verlorene Stadtbild von einst läßt sich nie ganz abtöten. Melancholie mischt sich immer hinein.

Die Stadtbildlosigkeit wiederum kann auf eine eigene Bildersprache nicht verzichten. Und die ist sogar besonders ambitioniert und beschwörend. In ihr artikulieren sich Trauer, Ästhetisierungskraft, geschichtstheoretische Anstrengungen und – die Vitalität Berlins. Die Stadt bekennt sich zur ungeglätteten Tektonik ihrer historischen Brüche, zu den geologischen Verwerfungen ihrer Geschichte. Eine Ästhetik des rauhen Widerspruchs wird propagiert, die scheinbar nur widerspiegelt, was das Antlitz von Berlin zeigt. Denn es ist wahr: Wie in keiner Stadt sonst in Deutschland sind hier noch immer die Spuren und Verheerungen der Kriegskatastrophe, die Maschinengewehreinschüsse, die Narben der Granatsplitter und Flächenbrände ablesbar. Dazu passen Definitionen wie: Berlin ist rüde, grell, laut, auftrumpfend und exzentrisch. Die Stadt versteht sich als Ort der Minderheiten, Abweichungen und Zweideutigkeiten, als ein Terrain der Subkulturen, der Szenen, alternativen Milieus, Nischen und Sekten.

Der Gegensatz könnte kaum extremer ausfallen, wenn man die Bildsprache Manfred Hamms mit dieser Ikonographie Berlins vergleicht. Beide Bildwelten dementieren sich radikal: Auf der einen Seite Achsen, Veduten, Portale, Kuppeln, Museen, Bibliotheken, Fassadengliederungen, Säulengänge, gestaltete Natur, Treppeninszenierungen, historische Perspektiven – Berlin als versteinerter Prozeß einer bürgerlichen Bildung, ergänzt durch Einblicke in Künstlerateliers, Cafés und Theater. Auf der anderen Seite das „penible Konglomerat" (Joseph Roth) wilder Kontraste und surrealistischer Traumlandschaften: der verfallene Stuck, die zerbrochenen Fassaden, die brandgeschwärzten Putten, die Einsamkeit von Betondurchgängen, die überwachsenen Geleise, die leerstehenden Fabrikhallen und Gasometer, die Currywurstkioske unter den S-Bahn-Bögen, die innerstädtischen Stadtbrachen, die ausrangierten Sofas am Wasser, die Gaststätten in der Ruine, die Intimität der Eckkneipen, die Tristesse der Wohnsilos mit ihren Grafitti und die diffuse

this self-interpretation is defended with great intensity. One senses the great effort of a city that has been thrown off course by history and sees itself as doomed to be different from other cities. There is also a sense of having relinquished something, and the nagging pain caused by the loss of the old city image cannot be completely eradicated. There is always a tinge of melancholy.

However, the lack of a city image cannot, in turn, do without its own visual language, and in this case it is a particularly ambitious and evocative one. In it sadness, the power of aestheticisation, historico-theoretical endeavours are expressed and – the vitality of Berlin. The city acknowledges the violent tectonics of its historical caesuras, the geological deformations of its history. An aesthetics of raw contradiction is propagated, which merely seems to reflect what is shown on the face of Berlin. For it is true: here, more than in any other city in Germany, the traces and devastation of the war are still clearly visible, the pock-marks left by machine gun bullets, the scars caused by grenade splinters and infernos. In keeping with this is the notion of Berlin as rude, brash, loud, swaggering and eccentric. The city sees itself as a place of minorities, deviations and ambivalence, as a terrain of subcultures, alternative milieus, niches and sects.

The contrast could hardly be more extreme when one compares Manfred Hamm's visual language with this iconography of Berlin. The two worlds of images contradict one another radically: on the one hand, axes, vedute, portals, domes, museums, libraries, rows of façades, colonnades, designed green spaces, stairways as architectural stagings, historical perspectives – Berlin as a petrified example of bourgeois cultivation, complemented by views into artists' studios, cafés and theatres. On the other hand, the "pernickety conglomeration" (Joseph Roth) of wild contrasts and surrealistic dreamscapes: the dilapidated stucco, the crumbling façades, the fire-blackened cherubs, the loneliness of the concrete passageways, the overgrown tracks, the disused factory buildings and gasometers, the snack-food kiosks under the railway bridges, the inner-city wasteland, the discarded sofas on the water's edge, the bars amidst the ruins, the intimacy of the corner pubs, the desolation of the mass housing blocks with their graffiti and the diffuse emptiness of modern urban spaces. Of course the classical and baroque ensembles of historical Berlin are also part of this picture, but merely as a fragmented backdrop that shimmers behind the contemporary scene, or as a quotation amidst the conglomeration. And everywhere, one encounters the wild-growing bushy outcrops of nature, which are among Berlin's specialities. This natural growth has taken over the disused areas in the city's centre, thrives in the no-man's land areas of the inner city, and, until only recently, trees grew out of church domes on the Gendarmenmarkt. This might lead one to reflect that the struggle between the urban world and untamed nature is not yet over. At any rate, urban society in Berlin exhibits analogies to this prolific natural vegetation. Berlin hardly presents itself as a

Leere der modernen Stadträume. Selbstverständlich gehören auch die klassizistischen und barocken Ensembles des historischen Berlins dazu, allerdings nur als Folie im Hintergrund, die bruchstückhaft hinter der Gegenwart hervorscheint, oder als Zitat im Konglomerat. Überall aber trifft man auf die herein- und hervorbrechende wildwachsende buschige Natur. Diese Natur gehört zu den Berliner Spezialitäten. Sie hat sich die Brachflächen im Zentrum erobert, gedeiht im innerstädtischen Niemandsland, und noch vor kurzem wuchsen Bäume aus den Kuppeln des Gendarmenmarktes. Da kann der Gedanke aufkommen, daß der Streit zwischen urbaner Welt und wilder Natur noch nicht ganz ausgestanden ist. Die Stadtgesellschaft jedenfalls zeigt Analogien zu dieser wuchernden vegetativen Natürlichkeit. Berlin präsentiert sich kaum als Ort urbaner Wohlerzogenheit, sondern mit Vorliebe als Agglomeration sozialer Biotope. Es ist die Stadt der Existenzen und des Alltagsexistentialismus.

Brandwand. Im Zentrum dieser Ikonographie des Fragments aber steht die Brandwand. Sie ist das geheime Siegel, das Stadtsymbol, das mit seiner haptischen Flächigkeit selbst schon eine Real-Abstraktion ist. Die Brandwände, das sind die Taktgeber der chaotischen Bildkollisionen. Was auch immer Berlin an Perspektiven, Achsen, Veduten, Fassadenabwicklungen tatsächlich noch besitzt, es wird fragmentiert und annihiliert durch die Flächigkeit der geschwärzten, ziegelroten oder grauen Brandwände. Sie lösen die Dreidimensionalität, die räumliche und geschichtliche Tiefe der Stadtansicht auf und lassen eine Melancholie der leeren Fläche und steinernen Femdheit übrig. (Manfred Hamm benutzt die Metapher der Brandwand nicht.) Was bedeutet die Brandwand? Sie ist das Zeichen der aufgebrochenen Stadt. Die feste Haut der Fassaden ist zerrissen, das Mauerwerk, das Skelett ist freigelegt. Oft zeichnen sich die Schatten abgerissener und zerstörter Häuser ab, Erinnerungen an das, was einmal Stadt war.

Die Ästhetik der Brandwand wurde schnell entdeckt. Werner Heldt nutzte sie unmittelbar nach Kriegsende als Metapher. Vielleicht war es auch die Magie der Brandwand, die der bildenden Kunst in Berlin immer eine realistische Stadtgebundenheit verlieh. Die Brandwand selbst bedeutet die Negation des Stadtbildes. Ihre zeitlose Präsenz erklärt alle Veduten, historischen Perspektiven und Fassaden zu ephemeren Erscheinungen. Sie waren die prädestinierten Opfer der Geschichte. Die Brandwand hingegen überlebte und symbolisiert das Überleben selbst. Sie verkündet, daß die Stadt bleibt.

Magie. Auch die Häßlichkeit der Brandwände ist eine Wahrheit der Stadt. Und ausdauernde Liebe hat es fertiggebracht, die Schönheit des häßlichen Berlin zu sehen. Diese Liebesarbeit muß man achten: Kein Zweifel, in dieser Stadt-

well-mannered urban environment, but rather as an agglomeration of social biotopes. It is the city of existences and everyday existentialism.

Fire wall. *However, it is the fire wall – or Brandwand – the expanse of windowless brick or concrete visible on the side of many buildings throughout Berlin, which occupies the central place in this iconography. It is the secret seal, the city symbol that, with its haptic surface structure, is itself a concrete abstraction. The fire walls dictate the rhythm of the chaotic collisions between images. Whatever Berlin still actually possesses in terms of perspectives, axes, vedute and façades is fragmented and annihilated by the blackened, brick-red or grey fire walls. They dissolve the three-dimensionality, the spatial and historical depth of the view the city presents, leaving nothing but the melancholy of empty space and stony strangeness. (Manfred Hamm does not use the metaphor of the fire wall.) What does the fire wall signify? It is the sign of the fragmented city. The firm skin of the façades has been torn away to reveal the naked brickwork, the skeleton. Often the shadowy traces of demolished or destroyed buildings are still visible, memories of what was once part of a city.*

The aesthetic of the fire wall was soon discovered. Werner Heldt employed it as a metaphor immediately following the end of the war. Perhaps it was the magic of the fire wall that lent post-war art in Berlin a realistic proximity to the city. The fire wall itself signifies a negation of the city image. Its timeless presence pronounces all vedute, historical perspectives and façades to be ephemeral manifestations. They were the predestined victims of history. The fire wall, however, survived and symbolises survival itself. It proclaims that the city remains.

Magic. *The ugliness of the fire wall is also a reality of the city. And enduring love has managed to see the beauty of ugly Berlin. One must respect this labour of love: there is no doubt that magic lies hidden in this city image of fire walls. For a long time now this image of the imageless city has been one of Berlin's winning attractions and successful exports. This is witnessed by the incessant production of photographic volumes, Berlin specials, issues of journals devoted to the city and city guides. Berlin's romanticism of the fragment and the melancholy of modernity have made the city the privileged setting for the contemporary novel. Berlin is a fashionable location for crime stories and television series. The* genius loci *create an expectation of abysses, eccentricity and the chance event that changes into destiny. Loneliness and madness, hopelessness and vitality are all part of this constellation. And the city of fragments (initially) finds the "New Berlin" very much to its liking. The city image of cranes and building sites that delve down to ice-age foundations heightens the magic still further. Lifestyle stagings, fashion presentations, product marketing, manifestations of the new luxury and even the new political scene, which has dubbed itself the "Berlin gen-*

landschaft der Brandwände steckt Magie. Das stadtbildlose Stadtbild ist seit langem ein Erfolgsprogramm und Exportschlager Berlins. Davon zeugt die anhaltende Flut von Photobänden, Berlin-*Specials*, Sonderheften und Stadtführern. Mit ihrer Romantik des Fragments und ihrer Melancholie der Moderne ist die Stadt zum privilegierten Ort des jungen Romans geworden. Als Schauplatz für Kriminalstories und Kriminalserien im Fernsehen ist Berlin *en vogue*. Der *genius loci* verspricht Abgründe, Exzentrik und jenen Zufall, der ins Schicksal umschlägt. Einsamkeit und Verrücktheit, Hoffnungslosigkeit und Vitalität passen dazu. Und die Stadt des Fragments verträgt sich (zunächst) blendend mit dem „neuen Berlin". Die Stadtlandschaft der Kräne und Baugruben, die zum eiszeitlichen Urgrund durchstoßen, steigert noch die Magie. *Lifestyle*-Inszenierungen, Modepräsentationen, Produktmarketing, Auftritte des neuen Luxus und selbst die junge Politik, die sich „Generation Berlin" nennt, beuten erfolgreich diesen Kontrast aus. Ohnehin hat die Grundstimmung der Stadt, jene Mischung aus Endzeit und Avantgarde, immer die jungen Kreativen angezogen (während die etablierten Künstler die Stadt verließen). Berlin ist ein Sonderfall, weil im Unterschied zu anderen Metropolen die Verwandlung verfallener Industrieareale und populärer Viertel in Zonen der Avantgarde und der kreativen Szene im Grunde die ganze Stadt erfaßt.

Aber auch wenn die Moden sich der Kultur des Fragments angenommen haben, ist an dieser Kultur nichts Modisches. Die Sichtweise Berlins als zersplitterte und melancholische Stadt liest sich nicht zufällig auch als Programmatik der Kunst-Avantgarde. Die Berliner Stadtlandschaft verkörpert geradezu die Ästhetik der Zersplitterung. Hier vermischen und steigern sich die urbane Realität und der dekonstruktivistische Diskurs. Berlin ist ein real existierendes dekonstruktivistisches Fanal. Die kalte Explosion historisch wichtiger Orte in der Stadt ist so radikal, daß die Bauten des Dekonstruktivismus wie das Jüdische Museum von Daniel Libeskind ihren Sinn völlig umkehren und nun Harmonie stiften.

II. Schönheit in stadtbürgerlicher Absicht

Die europäische Stadt und das Stadtbild. Die Frage ist also, was an diesem Konsens der Stadtbildlosigkeit eigentlich falsch sein soll und was beklagenswert. Berlin hat schließlich aus dem sinistren Reiz des Fragmentarischen eine Erfolgsgeschichte gemacht. Ist die Rede vom Stadtbild, die Klage über den Verlust nicht nur Nostalgie? Wäre also Manfred Hamms Klassizität nichts als hilflose Beschwörung einer für immer vergangenen Geschichte? Aber wenn Berlin so gut ohne die Autorität eines Stadtbildes leben kann, wenn die Stadt mit

eration," is successfully exploiting this contrast. The prevailing mood of the city, that mixture of closing act and avant-garde, has in any case always attracted young creative people (whereas established artists have tended to leave the city). Berlin is a special case, because in contrast to other major cities the transformation of dilapidated industrial areas and popular districts into zones of the avant-garde and the artistic scene basically applies to the entire city.

However, even if fashion has adopted the culture of the fragment, there is nothing fashionable about this culture. It is no coincidence that Berlin's view of itself as a splintered and melancholic city can also be read as programmatic for the artistic avant-garde. The Berlin city image virtually embodies the aesthetic of fragmentation. Here urban reality and deconstructive discourse mingle and intensify. Berlin is a practically existing deconstructive signal. The callous explosion of historically important locations in the city is so radical that deconstructivist buildings such as the Jewish Museum by Daniel Libeskind completely reverse their meaning and now create harmony.

II. Beauty as the intention of the citizenry

The European city and the city image. *The question is thus whether there is anything wrong with or regrettable about this consensus on the absence of a city image. After all, Berlin has made a success story out of the sinister charm of the fragmentary. Might not all this talk of the city image, the lamenting of its loss, be simply nostalgia? Could Manfred Hamm's classicism be nothing more than a helpless evocation of a history that is gone forever? But if Berlin is able to do so well without the authority of a city image, if the city can succeed with its culture of the fragment and the caesura, why is it that whenever the question of the city image is raised, it immediately gives rise to confused ideological debates on topics ranging from architecture, urban form, town planning and historical interpretation to the smouldering East-West conflict? Why are so many intellectuals convinced that Berlin's identity can be sought in any number of fields, but definitely not in its city image? Why is this question considered inappropriate, superfluous? The concept of the city image clearly seems to be an emotive one that touches on a taboo.*

It has been said that Manfred Hamm's photographs are a portal; in fact they lead, even seduce, the observer to really think about the city and, in particular, to reflect on its eccentricity. This process begins with the deceptively mundane concept of city image. Applied to the European city, the phrase "every city has a city image" ought to constitute a simple, almost tautological statement. Here, the city image is never regarded as a mere sum of pleasant views and is always more than the contents of the postcard stand outside the imaginary newspaper kiosk. Understood as an ideal, it is the character, the aesthetic programme,

ihrer Kultur des Fragments und der Brüche reüssiert, warum gerät man dann sogleich in unübersichtliche ideologische Debatten um Architektur, Stadtgestalt, Stadtplanung, Geschichtsverständnis bis hin zum schwelenden Ost-West-Konflikt, wenn die Frage des Stadtbildes berührt wird? Warum sind so viele Intellektuelle davon überzeugt, daß Berlins Identität in allen möglichen Bereichen, aber keinesfalls im Stadtbild gesucht werden darf? Warum gilt die Frage danach als unangemessen, überflüssig? Der Begriff des Stadtbildes ist offenbar ein Reizwort und trifft ein Tabu.

Die Photographien von Manfred Hamm seien ein Portal, wurde gesagt; tatsächlich führen und verführen sie dazu, grundsätzlich über Stadt nachzudenken und insbesondere die Exzentrizität Berlins zu reflektieren. Das beginnt mit diesem so selbstverständlichen Wort Stadtbild: Der Satz „jede Stadt hat ein Stadtbild“ sollte für die europäische Stadt eine einfache, fast tautologische Gleichung sein. Das Stadtbild wird dabei nie nur als eine Summe schöner Ansichten begriffen und ist immer mehr als der Postkartenständer vor dem imaginären Kiosk. Wenn man es als Ideal versteht, so ist es die Prägung, das ästhetische Programm, nach dem sich die Stadt auch in Zukunft formen will. Ein Kanon, eine langsam herausgebildete Ikonographie, die Einverständnis und Verpflichtung der Stadtbürger gegenüber dem Gemeinwesen darstellt. Es gehört zum Wesen der europäischen Stadt, daß ihr Bild nicht einfach entstand, sondern in kontinuierlichen Auseinandersetzungen geschaffen wurde. Im Stadtbild wurden die Glanzzeiten verewigt, die Gunst der Topographie gestaltet, die wirtschaftliche Bedeutung gefeiert. Wir begegnen urbanen Inszenierungen, gebauten Machtansprüchen, Versteinerungen der Individualität der Städte und sehen die Zeichen einer permanenten Selbstdarstellung der Stadtgesellschaft. Das Stadtbild erzählt die Geschichte der Stadt. Aber welche Geschichte kann, soll und darf Berlin erzählen?

Die Fischerinsel und ihre Umgebung 1940, 1953, 1989, 2000
The area around the Fischerinsel 1940, 1953, 1989, 2000

according to which the city aspires to form itself in the future as well. It is a canon, a slowly elaborated iconography that represents the consent and obligation of the citizens in regard to the community. It is part of the essence of the European city that its image has not simply emerged, but has been created in a process of continual debate. In the city image the highpoints of the city's development have been preserved, its topographical appeal shaped, its economic significance celebrated. We encounter stagings of urban existence, constructed claims to power, petrifications of the individuality of the city, and the signs of a self-portrayal of urban society. The city image tells the history of the city. But what history can, should and may Berlin tell?

Embellishment. *City images emerge from a continuum of etched views, panoramas, vedute, biographies, travel accounts, poems, songs and memories. The ideas of the time are articulated in the city image. The ideal city of the Renaissance with its central perspective broke with the naturally evolved medieval city. Baroque embellishment linked the city with the stagings of the absolutist court. Honorary titles such as "Athens on the Spree," "Florence on the Elbe," "Venice of the North," are witness to the hierarchies and pretensions of European city images. The large-scale destruction of cities by fire and war was never followed merely by pragmatic restoration but always the construction of a more beautiful city. The city image is thus shaped not only by the representation of the city's history, but also the continually reinterpreted aspiration to beauty.*

The first half of the nineteenth century saw the major capitalist cities become shockingly conspicuous with their mass populations, slums and increasing traffic, and as a result this period also saw the development of an organisational and aesthetic reaction in the form of the boulevards. They were the instrument with which the medieval infrastructure of the city centres were broken up and modernised. Upon the demolished embankments and ramparts, the metropolitan cities created the stage for their self-portrayal, and presented a new figure as actor and arbiter ele-

Embellissement. Stadtbilder wachsen aus einem Kontinuum gestochener Stadtansichten, Panoramen, Veduten, Reisebeschreibungen, Biographien, Gedichten, Liedern und Erinnerungen. Die Ideen der Zeit artikulieren sich im Stadtbild. Die ideale Stadt der Renaissance mit ihrer Zentralperspektive brach mit der naturwüchsigen mittelalterlichen Stadt. Das *Embellissement* des Barocks verknüpfte die Stadt mit den Inszenierungen des absolutistischen Hofes. Ehrentitel wie Spreeathen, Elbflorenz, Venedig des Nordens verraten Rangordnungen und Ansprüche europäischer Stadtbilder. Auf die großen Stadtzerstörungen durch Brände und Kriege folgte nie nur die pragmatische Wiederherstellung, sondern immer als Antwort der Bau der schöneren Stadt. Nicht nur die dargestellte Stadtgeschichte prägt also das Stadtbild, sondern auch der immer wieder neu interpretierte Anspruch auf Schönheit.

Als in der ersten Hälfte des 19. Jahrhunderts die kapitalistischen Metropolen mit ihren Menschenmassen, Elendsquartieren und dem aufkommenden Massenverkehr schockartig sichtbar wurden, entstand ein Gegenprogramm, eine organisatorische und ästhetische Reaktion: die Boulevards. Sie waren das Instrument, mit dem die mittelalterliche Infrastruktur der Stadtkerne aufgebrochen und modernisiert wurde. Auf den geschleiften Festungsringen und Wallanlagen schufen sich die Metropolen die Bühne für ihre Selbstdarstellung und präsentierten eine neue Figur als Akteur und *arbiter elegantiarum:* den Flaneur. Wie ein Kunstwerk ließ Baron Haussmann im Paris des zweiten Kaiserreichs die neuen Boulevards enthüllen – eine Zeremonie, die den Staatsakt und das neuartige Massenspektakel miteinander verband: die Inszenierung der Metropole als urbane Skulptur.

Das Berliner Stadtbild. Selbstverständlich kann sich auch Berlin auf seine Stadtbildgeschichte berufen, eine Geschichte bemerkenswerter Ambitionen. Die Verwandlung einer Residenz des ländlichen Barock zur Hauptstadt des Industriestaates Preußen und dann zur Kaiserstadt wurde von einer reichen Bildtradition getragen, von den biedermeierlich-klassizistischen Veduten eines Eduard Gaertner bis hin zu den impressionistischen Momenten der schnell wachsenden wilhelminischen Metropole in den Ölskizzen von Adolf Menzel. Aber Stadtbild und Schönheit entfalteten sich in Berlin nicht kontinuierlich nach Maßgabe der stadtgesellschaftlichen Entwicklung. Die Bürgerstadt, die Doppelstadt Berlin/Cölln, hatte früh schon, im Mittelalter, den Machtkampf mit der Landesherrschaft der Hohenzollern verloren, die selten Zuneigung für die Berliner Bürger zeigten und die Stadt oft als Kulisse höfischer Selbstdarstellung behandelten. Die jüngste Metropole Europas, der Parvenü gewissermaßen, war geprägt von schubartigen Wachstumssprüngen. Die friderizianische Residenzstadt verwandelte sich zum Ende

gantiarum – the flâneur. In the Paris of the Second Empire, Baron Haussmann had the new boulevards unveiled like an artwork – a ceremony which linked the state occasion with the modern mass spectacle: the staging of the metropolis as urban sculpture.

The Berlin city image. *Of course, Berlin can also refer to the history of its city image, a history of remarkable ambitions. The transformation of a rural baroque royal seat into the capital of the Prussian industrial state and then into the imperial city drew on a rich pictorial tradition – from the Biedermeier-classical vedute of an Eduard Gaertner to the impressionistic moments of the rapidly growing Wilhelminian metropolis in the oil studies of Adolf Menzel. However, the concepts of city image and beauty did not unfold continuously in Berlin according to the development of urban society. Already in the Middle Ages, the burgher city, the dual city of Berlin/Cölln, had lost its power struggle with the Hohenzollern dynasty, which seldom exhibited any affection for the Berlin burghers and often treated the city as the backdrop for displays of the power of its court. Europe's youngest metropolis, the parvenu so to speak, was shaped by jolting leaps of growth. At the end of the nineteenth century, the royal seat of Frederick the Great was explosively transformed into the leading centre of German industrial expansion. Its area and population increased fivefold in only a few decades. These powerful developmental jolts were also manifested in the changes to the city image. From the time of Frederick the Great onwards, the city shed its skin every thirty years and discarded its old image.*

Colonial city. *The radical revisions of the city image began with the miracle celebrated by Voltaire with the words "Sparta became Athens." From this point onwards, one can speak of a Berlin tradition of revising and replacing the old faces of the city. One often encounters the term "creative destruction" as denoting the typical characteristic of the* genius loci. *On the one hand, this shows the force of the ambitions at work. But it illustrates just as clearly how eagerly Berlin mobilised destructive energies in order to implant the prevailing notion of beauty. It was precisely this which characterised the "eternal colonial city" with its "young-old face," as the philosopher Ernst Bloch described the city on the river Spree in 1932. Its fate, as he saw it, was that it "is always in the process of becoming and never is." A "particularly Protestant harshness" ensued from the "prehistoric environment" in which the city developed. For Karl Scheffler, the great Berlin critic writing at the end of the nineteenth century, a powerful compulsion to shape, which often led to architectural monotony, derived from the fact that Berlin had emerged "far from the birthplaces of German culture" and "in the midst of this endless Eastern land."*

Precisely these theses of Scheffler and Bloch have today assumed a new significance for the way in which Berlin understands itself as a city and as a capital. Its destiny as a colonial

des 19. Jahrhunderts explosionsartig in die Industriemetropole und Gründerzeitstadt. Sie verfünffachte ihren Umfang und ihre Bevölkerung innerhalb weniger Jahrzehnte. Diese gewaltigen Entwicklungsschübe zeigten sich auch in der Stadtbildfolge: Seit Friedrich dem Großen häutete sich die Stadt jeweils im Abstand von dreißig Jahren und warf ihr altes Bild ab.

Kolonialstadt. Die radikalen Stadtbildrevisionen begannen mit dem Wunder, das Voltaire in den Worten „aus Sparta ward Athen" feierte. Seitdem kann man von einer Berliner Tradition sprechen, immer wieder die alten Stadtansichten zu revidieren und zu ersetzen. Es wird gern von der „schöpferischen Zerstörung" als typischem Merkmal des *genius loci* geredet. Das zeigt einerseits, wie stark die Ambitionen waren. Ebenso deutlich aber wird, wie bereitwillig Berlin destruktive Energien mobilisierte, um den zeitgenössischen Schönheitsbegriff zu implantieren. Gerade das kennzeichnet die „ewige Kolonialstadt" mit ihrem „jungalten Gesicht" – so nannte der Philosoph Ernst Bloch 1932 die Spreemetropole. Ihr Schicksal sei, daß sie „immer nur wird und nie ist". Eine „besonders protestantische Härte" ergebe sich aus der „prähistorischen Umgebung", in der die Stadt wuchs. Auch Karl Scheffler, der große Berlinkritiker am Ende des 19. Jahrhunderts, leitet eine gewaltsame Formungswut, die oft zur architektonischen Eintönigkeit führe, daraus ab, daß Berlin „weit ab von den Stammgebieten der deutschen Kultur" und „inmitten dieses endlosen Ostlands" entstand.

Gerade diese Thesen von Scheffler und Bloch haben heute für das Selbstverständnis als Stadt und Hauptstadt eine neue Bedeutung bekommen. Das Schicksal, als Kolonialstadt immer auch eine Stadt der Moderne sein zu müssen, wird jetzt unumwunden als Rechtfertigung der Nachkriegsmoderne und ihrer Abräumwut verstanden. Wie fragwürdig diese Apologie ist, wird noch erörtert werden. Aber eines erhellt dieser historische Exkurs: daß in Berlin die Frage nach dem Stadtbild traditionell ein großes Gewicht hatte.

Das wurde auch nicht durch die Industrie- und Mietskasernenstadt dementiert. Im Gegenteil. Berlin stand Pate für die Entdeckung der Schönheit der Großstadt in Deutschland. Der Jugendstilarchitekt August Endell bezieht sich in seinem programmatischen Essay über „die Schönheit der großen Stadt" (1913) ausdrücklich auf Berlin. Er schuf zugleich die „Hackeschen Höfe", deren funkelnde, in Blau und Orange glühende Arabesken zum Symbol des wiedergefundenen alten Berlins geworden sind. Endell definiert in seinem Essay die Schönheit der Metropole als die Schöpfung einer Kultur des Sehens, als impressionistische Vision, die ständig durch das Auge des Großstädters geschaffen wird. Die Kapitelüberschriften in diesem Essay lauten: „Die Geistigkeit des Sichtbaren", „Der Luftschleier", „Die Arbeitsschönheit". Wer

city to always have to be a city of modernity as well is now unreservedly understood as a justification for post-war modernity and its frenzy of clearing away. Just how questionable this apologia is will be discussed. However, what this historical digression does shed light on is the fact that in Berlin the issue of the city image has traditionally carried great weight.

The transformation of Berlin into an industrial and tenement city did not negate the significance of this issue. On the contrary, Berlin constituted the focal point for the discovery of the beauty of the City in Germany. In his programmatic essay on "The beauty of the large city" (1913) the Art Nouveau architect August Endell referred particularly to Berlin. It was also Endell who created the "Hackesche Höfe" complex, the glowing blue and orange arabesques of which have become a symbol of the rediscovered old Berlin. In his essay, Endell defined the beauty of the metropolis as the creation of a culture of seeing, as an impressionistic vision that is constantly created by the eye of the metropolitan inhabitant. The chapter headings in his essay are "The intellectuality of the visible," "The veil of air," "The beauty of work." Anyone wanting not only to survive but also live in the large city will seek its beauty and have to embrace a pride in its appearance. The fact that this claim of the city on its inhabitants and of the inhabitant on the city belongs to the concept of citizenship, is indeed constitutive of the community, was recognised most clearly ten years later by the most significant and charming of Berlin's flâneurs, the writer Franz Hessel. Strolling on Kurfürstendamm, he was delighted by the "southerning" of the city, and he even linked this to its political culture: for it was precisely in this character that he saw the promise of a "democratic urban optimism." Some seventy years later – following the Nazi period, the Second World War and the division of Berlin – the Berlin expert Dieter Hoffmann-Axthelm touched on this connection between beauty and urban cultural life, summarising as follows: "Beautiful is seeing what is considered as having to be seen."

Just how seriously the relationship between urban ways of life and and urban beauty is now being taken is illustrated by the urbanist debates concerning the metropolitan cities. These are no longer seen as Moloch and problem cases, but represent an ecologically sensible, resource-preserving way of life. In this understanding, beauty is also comprehended as a precondition for the sustainability of the urban structure. Thus, the city image was never and is still today not just a secondary aspect in the history of cities. It is common property, heritage, and a guarantee of a sophisticated way of life. In its tension between historical narration and beauty, the city image was the visible pledge of citizenship.

And so we pose the question again. The imageless Berlin, the biotope of the fragment and the eccentric, surely also possesses its own form of beauty and magic. Why then not accept that which emerged in the post-war period? The answer lies in the nature of

in der großen Stadt nicht nur überleben, sondern auch leben will, wird ihre Schönheit suchen und auf das Sich-sehen-lassen-können der Stadt nicht verzichten wollen. Daß dieser Anspruch der Stadt an den Einwohner und des Einwohners an die Stadt zur Stadtbürgerschaft gehört, ja konstitutiv für das Gemeinwesen ist, hat am schärfsten der bedeutendste und charmanteste Flaneur Berlins, der Schrifsteller Franz Hessel, zehn Jahre später erkannt. Bei seiner Flanage auf dem Kurfürstendamm entzückt ihn die „Versüdlichung" der Stadt, und er schlägt die Brücke selbst zur politischen Kultur: denn gerade darin sieht er die Verheißung eines „demokratischen Stadtfrohsinns." Rund siebzig Jahre später – die Nazizeit, der Zweite Weltkrieg und die Teilung Berlins liegen dazwischen – ertastet der Berlinkenner Dieter Hoffmann-Axthelm diesen Zusammenhang von Schönheit und städtischem Kulturleben. In nüchterner Verkürzung definiert er: „Schön ist, gesehen zu haben, was man gesehen haben muß."

Wie ernst mittlerweile die Beziehung von urbaner Lebensform und städtischer Schönheit genommen wird, zeigt die neue urbanistische Debatte über die Metropolen. Diese gelten nicht mehr als Moloch und Problemfall, sondern repräsentieren eine ökologisch sinnvolle, weil ressourcenschonende Lebensweise. In diesem Verständnis wird auch die Schönheit als eine Voraussetzung für die Nachhaltigkeit der urbanen Struktur begriffen. Das Stadtbild war also nie und ist auch heute nicht nur ein Nebenaspekt in der Geschichte der Städte. Es ist ein Gemeingut, ein Erbe, ein Garant einer anspruchsvollen Lebensform. In seiner Spannung zwischen historischer Narration und Schönheit war das Stadtbild das sichtbare Unterpfand der Stadtbürgerschaft.

Noch einmal fragen wir also: Das stadtbildlose Berlin, der Biotop der Fragmente und Exzentrik, besitzt doch auch seine Art der Schönheit und Magie. Warum also nicht akzeptieren, was in den Nachkriegsjahrzehnten entstand? Die Antwort liegt in der Natur des Fragments selbst. Zu ihm gehört untilgbar die Spur des verlorenen Stadtbildes. So attraktiv und provozierend der gegenwärtige Zustand der Stadt auch ist, eines kann die Kultur des Fragments nicht bieten: Dauer. Wer diese Kultur beschwört und ideologisiert, spricht im Grunde schon den Nachruf. Die gegenwärtige Konjunktur, die das Berlin der Brüche und Brandwände, ihre Vermarktung in alle Richtungen nutzt, trägt bereits den Keim des Wandels und des Abschieds in sich. Eine Stadt kann nicht für ewig auf den Anspruch eines Stadtbildes verzichten, so wenig wie sie den Stolz preisgeben kann.

Bildungsanspruch. Der Berliner Konsens der stadtbildlosen Stadt verweigert sich nicht nur diesen Zusammenhängen. Er gibt vor allem eines auf: den Bildungsanspruch, der in der urbanen *civitas* verkörpert wird. Ein Stadtbild stellt immer auch einen visuellen Anspruch auf Ausbildung des

the fragment itself, an indelible part of which is the trace of the lost city image. As attractive and provocative as the present condition of the city is, one thing that the culture of the fragment cannot offer is duration. Anyone who evokes and ideologises this culture is already speaking its obituary. The present economic situation, which is marketing the Berlin of caesuras and fire walls in all directions, already embodies the seed of change and leave-taking. A city cannot do without the claim to a city image forever, just as it cannot abandon its pride.

The claim to cultivation. *The Berlin consensus of the imageless city not only refuses to embrace these contexts. Above all it gives up the claim to cultivation embodied in urban* civitas. *A city image always represents a visual claim to the cultivation of taste and custom. It signals to the newcomer that one must behave and adapt to the style of public existence. When the Berlin essayist Karl Schlögel characterised the new European era following the epochal change with the motto of the "return of the cities," this is precisely what he was referring to: the re-establishment of European culture through the reconstruction of its urban civilisation. This applies to the cities of eastern Europe from Tallin to Lemberg; but it also applies to Germany's most eastern metropolitan city. Berlin is positioned precisely at the centre of this change. It must learn to see itself anew.*

III. The culture of the anomaly

Uniformity and trivialisation. *The renunciation of a city image cannot be adequately explained by referring only to the magic of the fragment and the fire wall. Concrete historical experiences must also be added to this constellation, and those of the post-war period are of enormous significance. Of course, in this period one can find enough efforts to define the city image, efforts that were in fact part of an intense East-West competitiveness. The two systems vied with one another: the "display window of the West," as Kurfürstendamm was called, competing with Stalinallee. The "twinkling West Berlin" (Witold Gombrowicz) had to shine and live. But it remained curiously superficial. The city as determinant of its image and role had abdicated and given itself over to the requirements of international politics: the four-sector city, the city of the Blockade, of the Cold War, of the Wall. Under the strain of international politics the great aggregation of people lived with quite non-specific, trivial claims to a comfortable modern apartment – a creeping impoverishment of the urban began.*

"Berlin is many cities." This famous sentence comes from Werner Düttmann, the architect of the Berlin Akademie der Künste, creator of the gargantuan Märkisches Viertel, and city architect in West Berlin from 1960 to 1966. He wrote: "Berlin is many places, places which the people gather in but do not become conscious of as space. If these places are immaterial, that is, all of them are regarded as the same, are without any particular

Geschmacks und der Sitten dar. Es signalisiert dem Neuling, daß man sich benehmen und dem Stil der Öffentlichkeit anpassen muß. Wenn der Berliner Essayist Karl Schlögel die neue Epoche Europas nach der Zeitenwende unter das Motto der „Wiederkehr der Städte" stellt, so ist genau das gemeint: die Wiederherstellung der europäischen Kultur durch die Rekonstruktion ihrer städtischen Zivilisation. Das gilt für die Städte Osteuropas von Tallinn bis Lemberg; das gilt aber auch für die östlichste Metropole Deutschlands. Berlin steht genau an dieser Wende. Es muß sich neu sehen lernen.

III. Die Kultur der Anomalie

Gleichheit und Banalisierung. Der Verzicht auf ein Stadtbild kann allein mit der Magie des Fragments und der Brandwand nicht ausreichend erklärt werden. Es müssen reale historische Erfahrungen dazukommen. Die gab es in der Nachkriegszeit in erschreckender Dimension. Selbstverständlich lassen sich auch in jener Epoche genug Anstrengungen, ja eine scharfe Ost-West-Konkurrenz um das Stadtbild entdecken. Die Systeme wetteiferten, das „Schaufenster des Westens", der Kurfürstendamm, konkurrierte mit der Stalinallee. Das „Glitzerding Westberlin" (Witold Gombrowicz) mußte leuchten und leben. Aber das blieb seltsam äußerlich. Die Stadt als Souverän ihres Bildes und ihrer Rolle war abgetreten, war dem weltpolitischen Schauplatz gewichen: die Vier-Sektoren-Stadt, die Stadt der Blockade, des Kalten Krieges, der Mauer. Unterhalb der weltpolitischen Anspannung lebte die große Aggregation von Menschen mit ganz unspezifischen, trivialen Ansprüchen auf eine moderne bequeme Wohnung – es begann eine schleichende Verelendung des Urbanen.

„Berlin ist viele Städte". Dieser berühmte Satz stammt von Werner Düttmann, dem Architekten der Akademie der Künste und dem Schöpfer des gigantomanischen „Märkischen Viertels", von 1960 bis 1966 Senatsbaudirektor in West-Berlin. Er schreibt: „Berlin ist viele Orte, Orte, die den Menschen, die sich darin versammeln, als Raum nicht bewußt werden. Wenn diese Orte gleichgültig sind, das heißt doch wohl auch alle als gleich gelten, ohne besondere Physiognomie zum Beispiel, muß ihnen eine andere Kraft innewohnen, die sie bedeutsam macht für die vielen, die sich hier versammeln." Diese Kraft, das darf man unterstellen, ist der Berliner Überlebenstrotz. Aber was Düttmann beschreibt, ist ein irritierendes Bild einer Stadt der Gleichheit und der Gleichheit der Stadt.

Dieses Bild widerspricht keineswegs dem Kanon des Fragments und der Heterogenität. Beide Tendenzen sprechen gleichermaßen von der Abwesenheit höherer orientierender Ordnungsprinzipien. Tatsächlich ist das Nachkriegs-

physiognomy for example, there must be another force inherent in them which renders them significant for the many who gather in them." This force, one might say, is the stubborn will of the Berliners to survive. However, what Düttmann describes is an irritating image of a city of uniformity and the uniformity of the city.

This image by no means contradicts the canon of the fragmentary and the heterogeneous. Both tendencies refer to the absence of a higher ordering principle. In fact, post-war Berlin was in fact virtually a classless society. Aristocracy, bourgeoisie, the Bildungsbürgertum (the educated classes) and the proletariat no longer played a role within urban life and no longer shaped the urban space. The Bildungsbürgertum had been decimated by National Socialism and the annihilation of the Jews in Berlin. Now began "the trivialisation of Berlin," wrote the publisher Wolf Jobst Siedler, one of the last survivors of the old Berlin society, "which gradually took hold of the intellectual world. The writers were the first to leave, followed by the leading figures of the theatre and art world, who Berlin had always based its reputation on." The middle-class world became impoverished. In particular, West Berlin lost its large industries, and the headquarters of large concerns disappeared. West Berlin and East Berlin become heavily subsidised entities – cities "on drips". Only the public service continued to grow.

Uniformity and eccentricity. *It was not only the social hierarchies that paled into insignificance (or in East Berlin were liquidated without further ado.) The urban spatial hierarchy also dissolved. The ranking order of centre, boulevard, prosperous middle-class district, workers' district and periphery disappeared. The indiscriminate character of structural decay created a natural tolerance of formlessness. Here was space for experiments, subcultures, eccentricities and deviations of all kinds. Here was where the political movement of the late sixties organised itself and the protagonists of the new ways of life, the communards, lodged in the old apartments of the upper classes. Here the alternative lifestyle developed its rules. A society of minorities emerged, which was later referred to as the "third German entity" along with the Federal Republic and GDR. This situation was precisely complemented by the non-image of the city, the iconography of the fragment, the fire walls, the emptiness, the wild-growing outcrops of nature and the disused railway tracks – a sequence of pictures which sounds like an aesthetic programme of modern art or a product of free poetry. In economic terms, Berlin was the capital of the public service; in cultural terms it was the capital of melancholy.*

The Wall. *But there was a deeper reason for the conspicuous effort to maintain the culture of the fragment. It was also a form of compensation and immunisation for the concrete suffering caused by the division of the city. The Wall was doubly unacceptable: due to the chronic sense of powerlessness experienced by the*

berlin beinahe eine klassenlose Gesellschaft. Adel, Bourgeoisie, Bildungsbürgertum, Proletariat spielen keine städtische Rolle mehr und prägen auch nicht den Stadtraum. Das Bildungsbürgertum ist mit dem Nationalsozialismus und der Vernichtung der Berliner Juden untergegangen. Es begann bald „jene Banalisierung Berlins", schreibt einer der letzten Überlebenden der alten Berliner Gesellschaft, der Verleger Wolf Jobst Siedler, „die allmählich auch die intellektuelle Welt ergriff. Die Schriftsteller wanderten als erste ab, dann folgten jene Köpfe aus der Theater- und Kunstwelt, auf die sich Berlin immer berufen hat." Die bürgerliche Welt verarmte. Insbesondere West-Berlin büßte seine großen Industrien ein. Konzernverwaltungen verschwanden. West-Berlin und Ost-Berlin wurden zu hochsubventionierten Gebilden, zu Städten „am Tropf". Nur der öffentliche Dienst wuchs und wuchs.

Gleichheit und Exzentrik. Nicht nur die gesellschaftlichen Hierarchien verblaßten (oder wurden im Osten kurzerhand liquidiert), sondern auch die stadträumliche Hierarchie löste sich auf. Die Rangordnung von Zentrum, Boulevard, gutbürgerlichem Viertel, Arbeitergegend und Peri- pherie verschwand. Die Gleichgültigkeit des Strukturverfalls schuf eine naturwüchsige Toleranz der Gestaltlosigkeit: Hier war Raum für Milieus, Szenen, Experimente, Subkulturen, für Exzentrik und Abweichungen aller Art. Hier organisierte sich die 68er Bewegung, und die Protagonisten der neuen Lebensformen, die Kommunarden, nisteten sich in den großbürgerlichen Wohnungen ein. Hier entwickelte das alternative Leben seine Regeln. Es entstand eine Gesellschaft aus Minderheiten, die später als „dritter deutscher Zustand" neben der Bundesrepublik und der DDR gelten sollte. Dazu paßte präzis das Nicht-Stadtbild, die Ikonographie des Fragments, der Brandwände, der Leere, der wilden Natur und toten Geleise – eine Bildfolge, die wie ein ästhetisches Programm der modernen

Das Hansaviertel und seine Umgebung 1940, 1953, 1989, 2000
The area around the Hansaviertel 1940, 1953, 1989, 2000

entire society of the city, and due to the shame that it was this structure which dominated the image of Berlin throughout the world. As long as Berlin remained divided by the Wall and separated from its environs, the cult of the fragment was a part of survival. It provided immunisation against Wall sickness. The eccentricity typical of the city and the indifference were also a sign of defiance and lust for life. But this was easily able to turn into ideology and resentment when the city once again became an object of discussion in the context of the fall of the Wall in 1989. The East Berlin town planner Wolfgang Kil attributes excessive significance to the culture of the fragment from the post-war period and turns its against the newly unified Berlin: "For a whole generation, Berlin was a warning sign. Fifty years are enough in order to pass on the disaster created by the previous generation to their descendants not only as atonement but gradually also as the normality of the city's image. Berlin itself became less and less adverse to the ubiquity of the fragmentary, in which solitary figures barely recall lost networks of streets. The grotesque division by the Wall had intensified the ciphers of urban anomaly to the level of the surreal: periphery from both sides." This quotation gives one a sense of how strong the intellectual resentment of Berlin's self-reflection can be subsequent to the events of 1989. The city is forced into the role of memorial and pedagogical example. But such ideologisation is infertile and will die out.

No-man's land. *One thing the normality of an "anomaly intensified to the level of the surreal" could certainly not be was a theme of preservation or a constructive maxim. For this normality had a precondition, a humus, which could only be found in walled-in Berlin: no-man's land. The empty zones on either side of the Wall were an inner-city periphery in the midst of the centre, an inner margin of emptiness. When the Wall fell, no-man's land became fertile. The petrified collision zones of the international blocs liquefied, bubbled and produced phantasmagoria.*

Kunst oder ein Produkt der freien Lyrik klingt. Ökonomisch gesehen war Berlin die Hauptstadt des öffentlichen Dienstes; kulturell war es die Hauptstadt der Melancholie.

Die Mauer. Aber es gibt noch einen tieferen Grund für das auffällige Bemühen, die Kultur des Fragments aufrechtzuerhalten: Es war auch eine Art Kompensation und Immunisierung gegen das reale Leiden an der Teilung der Stadt. Die Mauer war doppelt unannehmbar: wegen der chronischen Erfahrung von Ohnmacht der Stadtgesellschaft insgesamt und wegen der Scham, daß es dieses Bauwerk ist, welches das Bild Berlins in der Welt prägt. Solange Berlin durch die Mauer zerschnitten und vom Umland abgetrennt war, gehörte der Kult des Fragments zum Überleben. Er immunisierte gegen die Mauerkrankheit. Die ortstypische Exzentrik und die Gleichgültigkeit waren dann auch ein Zeichen des Trotzes und der Lebenslust.

Aber das konnte schnell in Ideologie und Ressentiment umschlagen, als die Stadt in ihrem Zusammenhang nach dem Mauerfall wieder auf die Tagesordnung kam. Das war im Jahre 1989. Der Ost-Berliner Stadtplaner Wolfgang Kil überhöht die Kultur des Fragments aus der Nachkriegszeit und wendet sie gegen das neu vereinte Berlin: „Berlin war eine Generation lang Europas Menetekel geblieben. Fünfzig Jahre reichen aus, um das von den Vätern angerichtete Desaster den Nachkommen nicht nur als Sühne, sondern allmählich auch als stadtbildliche Normalität zu vermitteln. Berlin selbst haderte immer weniger mit seiner Allgegenwart des Fragementarischen, in der einsame Solitäre verlorengegangene Straßennetze kaum mehr memorieren. Der groteske Mauerschnitt hatte die Chiffren städtischer Anomalie geradezu ins Surreale gesteigert: Peripherie von beiden Seiten." Das Zitat läßt erahnen, wie stark das intellektuelle Ressentiment gegen die Selbstbesinnung Berlins nach 1989 sein kann. Der bessere Deutsche oktroyiert der Stadt die Rolle als Mahnmal und Geschichtslehrpfad auf. Aber solche Ideologisierungen sind unfruchtbar und werden absterben.

Niemandsland. Die Normalität einer „ins Surreale gesteigerten Anomalie" konnte eines gewiß nicht sein: ein Thema der Bewahrung oder eine konstruktive Maxime. Denn diese Normalität hatte eine Voraussetzung, einen Humus, den es allein im ummauerten Berlin gab: das Niemandsland. Die leere Zone zu beiden Seiten der Mauer war eine innerstädtische Peripherie mitten im Zentrum, ein innerer Rand der Leere. Als die Mauer fiel, wurde das Niemandsland fruchtbar. Die erstarrten Kollisionszonen der Weltblöcke verflüssigten sich, warfen Blasen, produzierten Phantasmagorien. Über Nacht erhob sich gegenüber dem düsteren, kuppellosen Reichstag ein riesiges Tor, zusammengeschweißt aus NVA-Panzerwagen. Ein rosaroter T-52-Panzer kroch über Mauerreste. Aus Mig-19-Düsenjägern enstanden Installatio-

Overnight, a huge gate, welded together from old East German army tanks rose opposite the sombre, domeless Reichstag. A pink T-52 tank crept over the remains of the Wall. Installations were created from Mig-19 jet fighters – no-man's land as a place of artistic armaments conversion. The systemic borders mutated into the artist's studio. Art nomads, alternative lifestylers had set up camp along what was once the Wall. Once again the anomaly of Berlin manifested itself and bore the surreal.

But then things moved rapidly. The first settlers in no-man's land, the art nomads, were driven out by the planners, the excavators, pile-drivers and cranes. The new district around Potsdamer Platz began to shoot up. In the bend in the river Spree, the great bar of concrete between the offices of the chancellor and the parliamentary buildings began to take shape. No-man's land dissolved. Now, following the emergence of a new Berlin with a government quarter, a business and entertainment centre and a central railway station on the inner-city periphery, the gaze is now finally falling on the historic centre of the city. The historical moment has come to negotiate the relationship between the city's history, heritage, destruction and modernity. Berlin can no longer evade the issue – it must leave the cocoon of anomaly; it cannot merely ride the crest of the wave of initial euphoria, but must traverse the barrier of destruction in order to comprehend where it really stands.

IV. Utopia and destruction

The shock of Venice. *At present Berlin is regarded as the "magic city" in Europe. In the ten years since the fall of the Wall, the city has been transformed into a demiurgic landscape. The great breath of change is producing construction site spectacles, construction site rhetoric and cascades of superlatives. The city images cited above seem like counter-images. Neither the classicism of Manfred Hamm nor the natural city of the fragment is compatible with the new city in the midst of national capital delirium. Germany has gained centre stage, and everything is pushing its way onto the programme. "Everyone here is a newcomer," as György Konrád, the Hungarian dissident and writer and current president of the Berlin Akademie der Künste, has put it. And the young people of Europe have heard the news and are coming to try their luck.*

Is this then the new reality? Ten years after the fall of the Wall, the German pavilion at the architectural biennale in Venice presents a radical denial of the city in its phase of emergence. Its relationship to the sensuousness of the body and the present of a life is like that of an X-ray. A shockingly cold cartography of urban destruction presented – the history of Berlin on black plans.

Black plans. *These are plans which show only the existing buildings and exclude all parks, squares, streets and watercourses.*

nen – das Niemandsland als Ort der artistischen Rüstungskonversion. Die Systemgrenzen mutierten zum Kunstatelier. Kunstnomaden, Rollheimer, Aussteiger hatten entlang der einstigen Mauer ihre Zelte aufgeschlagen. Noch einmal kontrahierte sich die Anomalie Berlins und gebar Surreales.

Aber dann ging es schnell. Die ersten Siedler im Niemandsland, die Kunstnomaden, wurden von den Planern, den Baggern, Rammen und Kränen vertrieben. Das neue Viertel um den Potsdamer Platz wuchs in die Höhe. Im Spreebogen nahm der große Betonriegel zwischen Kanzleramt und Parlamentsbauten Gestalt an. Das Niemandsland löste sich auf. Jetzt, nachdem sich in der innerstädtischen Peripherie ein neues Berlin mit Regierungsviertel, Geschäfts- und Unterhaltungszentrum und Zentralbahnhof abzeichnet, fällt nun endlich der Blick auf das historische Zentrum der Stadt. Der geschichtliche Augenblick ist gekommen, über das Verhältnis von Stadtgeschichte, Erbe, Zerstörung und Moderne zu verhandeln. Berlin kann nun nicht mehr ausweichen – es muß den Kokon der Anomalie verlassen; es kann nicht nur auf dem Wellenkamm der Aufbruchstimmung schweben, sondern muß auch den Bannkreis der Zerstörung abschreiten, um zu begreifen, wo es wirklich steht.

IV. Utopie und Zerstörung

Der Schock von Venedig. Berlin gilt gegenwärtig als die „magic city" in Europa. In den zehn Jahren nach dem Fall der Mauer hat sich die Stadt in ein demiurgisches Gefilde verwandelt. Der große Atem der Veränderung treibt Baustelleninszenierungen, Baustellenrethorik und Kaskaden von Superlativen hervor. Wie Gegenbilder wirken da die oben zitierten Stadtbilder. Weder die Klassizität Manfred Hamms noch die Naturstadt des Fragments passen zu der neuen Stadt im Hauptstadtdelirium. Deutschland hat eine Zentralbühne bekommen, und alles drängt sich in den Spielplan. „Jeder ist hier Neuling", das ist die Formel des ungarischen Dissidenten und Schriftstellers György Konrád, der gegenwärtig als Präsident der Akademie der Künste amtiert. Und die Jugend Europas hat die Botschaft vernommen und kommt, um ihr Glück zu suchen.

Ist das nun die neue Wirklichkeit? Zehn Jahre nach dem Fall der Mauer zeigt der deutsche Pavillon auf der Architekturbiennale in Venedig ein radikales Dementi zu jener Stadt im Aufbruch. Es verhält sich zur Sinnlichkeit des Leibes und zur Gegenwart eines Lebens wie eine Röntgenaufnahme. Eine schockierend kalte Kartographie der Stadtzerstörung wird präsentiert – die Geschichte Berlins auf Schwarzplänen.

Schwarzpläne. Es sind Pläne, die in schwarzer Kontur allein die vorhandenen Bauten zeigen, unter Weglassung aller Parks, Plätze, Straßen und Wasserläufe. Auch wer Ber-

Even those who are not familiar with Berlin can see an alarming and highly dramatic mutation of the urban body. The pre-war situation is shown by the clearly defined historical developmental pattern of the city. There is the medieval small-scale, unstructured core of the dual city of Berlin/Cölln. This is followed by the clarity and rationality of the baroque extensions of the city with the wreath of squares, the Quarré (Pariser Platz), the Octogon (Leipziger Platz) and the Rondell (Mehringplatz) – a tableau of logical beauty. The next layer is the enormous city of the nineteenth century, with its boulevard rings and its large housing blocks, in which the courtyards are arranged behind one another: the city of the Wilhelminian bourgeoisie, which was also the city of the tenement blocks. The black plan of 1953 still reveals the historical layout of the city at a time in which many damaged buildings had been cleared away or blown up. It is evident that this layout had survived the war. The bombs and street battles had destroyed or damaged seventy per cent of the buildings, but not the city image.

However, in the fifties a process of uncanny decay begins, an infestation of metastases of annihilation. Structures disappear. The medieval centre dissolves and displeasingly large buildings, incompatible with the traditional dimensions subvert the texture. Particularly in East Berlin, in the historical centre, decay causes havoc. It is an unsettling X-ray of Berlin, one that by no means shows only the transformation of the historical ground plan, but the destruction of the city on a gigantic scale. The historical centre, which in the GDR mutated into the governmental centre of modern socialism, was extensively depopulated, losing in the process two thirds of its pre-war population. These extensive and tenacious urban negations induce a shudder, revealing as they do a shameful truth. Was this destructive furore the reality of Berlin? Why is it precisely now that these black plans present us with such a pessimistic viewpoint? This has nothing to do with hidden masochism. It is rather the beginning of a new way of seeing. Berlin must first recognise how far it was driven away from its own history, the history of its plots, buildings and the layout of its streets, in order to find its way back and to be able to begin the process of healing. One thing becomes clear here: such a system of destruction cannot originate from pure destructive rage. Other forces were at work, namely the energies of Good and a totalitarian reaching for the future. After the bombs came the utopias.

Light, air, sun. *In the beginning there was sunshine. The streets cleared of rubble served as the setting for the young and the new era. The new era held out the promise of the new city and vice versa. The propaganda picture of the construction of Stalinallee shows the young proletarian with rolled up sleeves who cheerfully pushes a wagon, while in the background we see the first outlines of the broad avenue. He is building the future and apartments into which he and those like him will move,*

lin nicht kennt, erblickt eine bestürzende und hochdramatische Mutation des Stadtkörpers. Der Vorkriegszustand zeigt das klar abgesetzte historische Entwicklungsmuster der Stadt. Der mittelalterliche kleinteilige, verwachsene Kern der Doppelstadt Berlin/Cölln. Es folgt die Clarté und Rationalität der barocken Stadterweiterungen mit dem Kranz der Plätze, dem Quarré (Pariser Platz), dem Octogon (Leipziger Platz) und dem Rondell (Mehringplatz) – ein Tableau logischer Schönheit. Die nächste Schicht ist die riesige Stadt des 19. Jahrhunderts, mit ihren Boulevardringen und ihren großen Wohnblöcken, in denen tief gestaffelt die Höfe liegen: die Stadt der wilhelminischen Bourgeoisie, die zugleich die Stadt der Mietskasernen war. Der Schwarzplan von 1953 zeigt zu einem Zeitpunkt, an dem schon viele beschädigte Gebäude abgeräumt oder gesprengt worden waren, noch immer das historische Stadtmuster. Es hatte, das ist evident, den Krieg überlebt. Die Bomben und die Straßenkämpfe hatten zwar etwa siebzig Prozent der Gebäude zerstört oder beschädigt, aber eben nicht das Stadtbild.

Mit den 50er Jahren aber beginnt eine unheimliche Zersetzung, ein Befall von Metastasen der Annihilation. Strukturen verschwinden. Das mittelalterliche Zentrum löst sich auf, und befremdlich große Gebäude, unvereinbar mit den traditionellen Maßstäben, zersetzen die Textur. Besonders in Ost-Berlin, in der historischen Mitte, wütet der Zerfall. Es ist ein beunruhigendes Röntgenbild von Berlin, das keineswegs nur die Transformation des historischen Grundrisses zeigt, sondern die Vernichtung von Stadt in riesigen Dimensionen. Die historische Mitte, in der DDR zum Staatszentrum des modernen Sozialismus mutiert, wurde regelrecht entvölkert, sie verlor zwei Drittel der Vorkriegsbevölkerung. Diese großflächigen und ausdauernden Stadtnegationen lassen frösteln, sie zeigen eine beschämende Wahrheit. War dieser destruktive Furor die Berliner Wirklichkeit? Warum lehren uns gerade jetzt die Schwarzpläne das Schwarzsehen? Mit

Der Spittelmarkt und seine Umgebung 1940, 1953, 1989, 2000
The area around the Spittelmarkt 1940, 1953, 1989, 2000

announces the accompanying text. "Free German youth, build," goes the hymn of the communist youth organisation. The blue shirt worn by its members bore the emblem of the rising sun. West Berlin's future was also bathed in sunshine. New buildings towered up from a landscape of high trees – Le Corbusier's Cité radieuse *as an upright, harmless suburban dream without a trace of radicalism. Traffic moved easily along broad roads, while overhead planes flew through a slightly cloudy sky.*

There was no space in these future idylls for the old Berlin, and the general optimism did not concern itself with the city's destruction. History had passed judgement. The fleets of bombers had carried it out. Condemned were the old society, the class society, National Socialism and thus the breeding ground of the nightmare world now gone – the old city. After so much destruction only the society of the free and equal could follow. Certainly the architects were free, in particular in their plans. The core dream of architectural modernity, the identity of a new society and new city was also dreamed of by the masses. The sea of debris only remained important insofar as it provided bricks.

In order to gauge the extremism and totalitarianism of these urban utopias, one must view the initial projects, which today seem merely absurd. Hans Scharoun, the first city architect following the war and renowned architect of the Berlin Philharmonic, radically liquidated the baroque layout of the city in his plan of 1947. He wanted to recreate Berlin in a banner formation issuing from the glacial valley. As Wolf Jobst Siedler later mocked: "History was replaced by geography. Scharoun elevated Neandertal man to the position of Berlin's general building director." As late as 1957 Scharoun published a vision of the inner city in which the buildings of the Prussian royal city, the Zeughaus, the Museumsinsel, the Deutsche and Französische Dom, the Bauakademie, are scattered as monuments over a green lawn. It is a vision that bears an alarming resemblance to the present city centre with its lawn laid over the foundations of the palace and the Bauakademie.

versteckter Masochismus hat dies nichts zu tun. Es ist vielmehr der Beginn eines neuen Sehens. Berlin muß erst erkennen, wie weit es von der eigenen Geschichte, der Geschichte seiner Grundstücke, Gebäude und Straßenmuster, weggetrieben war, um zurückfinden und die Heilung beginnen zu können. Eines wird dabei klar: Eine derartige Systematik der Zerstörung kann nicht aus der puren Zerstörungswut entspringen. Da waren andere Kräfte am Werk, nämlich die Energien des Guten und der totalitäre Griff nach der Zukunft. Nach den Bombern kamen die Utopien.

Licht, Luft, Sonne. Am Anfang war Sonnenschein. Die von Trümmern befreiten Straßen, das war der Schauplatz für die Jugend und die neue Zeit. Die neue Zeit versprach die neue Stadt und umgekehrt. Das Propagandabild vom Aufbau der Stalinallee zeigt den jungen Proletarier mit aufgekrempelten Ärmeln, der fröhlich die Lore schiebt, im Hintergrund die erste Kontur der breiten Allee. Er baut die Zukunft und Wohnungen, in die er und seinesgleichen einziehen werden, verkündet der Text. „Freie deutsche Jugend, baut auf", hieß es in der Hymne der kommunistischen Jugendorganisation. Auf ihrem blauen Hemd war das Emblem der aufgehenden Sonne. Auch West-Berlins Zukunft war sonnenüberflutet. Aus einer Landschaft hoher Bäume ragten die Neubauten – Le Corbusiers *Cité radieuse* als biederer, harmloser Vorstadttraum ohne eine Spur von Radikalität. Auf breiten Autostraßen flutete ungehindert der Verkehr, und im leicht bewölkten Himmel kreuzten die Flugzeuge.

In diesen Zukunftsidyllen gab es keinen Raum für das alte Berlin, und der allgemeine Optimismus scherte sich nicht um seine Zerstörung. Das Urteil der Geschichte war gefällt. Die Bomberflotten hatten es vollstreckt. Verurteilt war die alte Gesellschaft, die Klassengesellschaft, der Nationalsozialismus und damit auch die Brutstätte der vergangenen Schreckenswelt, die alte Stadt. Nach soviel Untergang konnte nur die Gesellschaft der Freien und Gleichen kommen. Und frei waren allemal die Erbauer, insbesondere in ihren Plänen. Den Kerntraum der Architekturmoderne, die Identität von neuer Gesellschaft und neuer Stadt, träumten auch die Massen. Das Ruinenfeld der alten Stadt war nur noch Ziegellieferant.

Um den Extremismus und Totalitarismus dieser Stadtutopien auszumessen, muß man sich einmal die Anfangsprojekte ansehen, die heute nur noch absurd erscheinen. Hans Scharoun, der erste Stadtbaudirektor nach dem Kriege und berühmte Erbauer der Philharmonie, liquidierte in seinem Plan von 1947 radikal das barocke Stadtmuster. Er wollte das neue Berlin bandförmig aus dem Urstromtal neu erschaffen. Wolf Jobst Siedler höhnte später: „Historie wurde durch Erdkunde ersetzt. Scharoun erhob den Neandertaler zum Generalbaumeister Berlins." Noch 1957 veröffentlichte Scharoun

Destructive utopias. *The destroyed city was a welcome* tabula rasa, *a unique historical opportunity. Finally the fetters of the city structure, private property and plot borders had been eliminated. When Martin Wagner, the renowned city architect of the Weimar period who modernised Berlin and promoted the construction of housing estates, returned from Turkish exile and presented a reconstruction plan which proposed retaining seventy per cent of the city, he was not even given a hearing. The agenda for Berlin contained only new buildings.*

Architectural modernity presented itself as a programme of publicly hygienic denazification. The sunshine of the new individual, however, was already incubated in the depths of the nineteenth century. He stepped up out of the dark tenement buildings, damp proletarian apartments and narrow attics. He was part of the programme of the strengthening Social Democratic movement. The historical Berlin was characterised by the saying coined by the plebeian chronicler Heinrich Zille: one could kill a person with an apartment as with an axe. From a public hygiene point of view the largest "tenement housing city in the world" appeared to be the source of all evil. It was the class struggle set in stone, the struggle between bourgeois front house and proletarian backyard, between the first floor and the attic. The more this way of seeing took hold of the conceptual world of town planning, the more the historical city image as well as the Wilhelminian embellishment with its ornamental orgies were grasped as the masquerade of a sociopolitical scandal. The codex for this way of seeing was created by Werner Hegemann in his book "Das steinerne Berlin" (1930). He exposed the land profiteers and the bourgeoisie as the forces of disaster. Hegemann articulated the great motif that would be so forcefully realised fifteen years later: only genuine, that is social, town planning could save one from "German mania". The garden city which he demanded for the people was in his view the guarantee of a politics of peace. This marked the beginning of the hegemony of social policy in Berlin, to which town planning was also subordinated.

After 1945, Berlin was thus under the spell of radical utopias, which blended to form a unique explosive device: the flight from the National Socialist past into the new society, the functionalistic dream of the modern metropolis, the furore over public hygiene which suggested the time for dealing with causes had come. To this was added the utopia of the modern city, which guaranteed freely flowing traffic for all. Historical amnesia was the common thread. The planning of traffic routes and the construction of public housing could rely on the state fervour for seizing property. Neither ownership of land nor the city image could stop the new city. The anti-urban functional utopias of a Le Corbusier with his Plan Voisin *(1925) or a Ludwig Hilberseimer with his* City-Bebauung *(1927) found their historical context. The fact is too often overlooked that after 1945 only the workers' parties remained as formative forces; they governed in both East*

eine Vision der Innenstadt, in der die Bauten der preußischen Königstadt, das Zeughaus, die Museumsinsel, der Deutsche und der Französische Dom, die Bauakademie, als verstreute Monumente auf der grünen Wiese stehen. Das heutige Zentrum mit dem Rollrasen über den Fundamenten von Schloß und Bauakademie kommt dieser Vision bedenklich nahe.

Destruktive Utopien. Die zerstörte Stadt war die willkommene *tabula rasa*, die einzigartige historische Chance. Endlich waren die Fesseln der Stadtstruktur, des Privateigentums und der Grundstücksgrenzen gesprengt. Als Martin Wagner, der renommierte Stadtbaudirektor der Weimarer Zeit, der Berlin modernisierte und den Siedlungsbau vorantrieb, aus dem türkischen Exil zurückkehrte und einen Wiederaufbauplan präsentierte, wonach siebzig Prozent der Stadt erhalten werden konnten, wurde er nicht einmal angehört. Allein Neubau stand auf der Tagesordnung.

Die Architekturmoderne bot sich als Programm sozialhygienischer Entnazifizierung an. Der Sonnenschein des neuen Menschen wurde allerdings schon in den Tiefen des 19. Jahrhunderts ausgebrütet. Er stieg auf aus dunklen Mietskasernen, feuchten Proletarierwohnungen und engen Mansarden. Er war Programmpunkt der erstarkenden Sozialdemokratie. Für das historische Berlin galt der Spruch ihres plebejischen Chronisten Heinrich Zille: Man könne einen Menschen mit der Wohnung erschlagen wie mit der Axt. Im Lichte der Sozialhygiene erschien die größte „Mietskasernenstadt der Welt" als Quell allen Übels. Sie war der versteinerte Klassenkampf, der Kampf zwischen bourgeoisem Vorderhaus und proletarischem Hinterhof, zwischen Beletage und Mansarde. Je mehr diese Sichtweise die stadtplanerische Ideenwelt ergriff, desto mehr wurde das historische Stadtbild und selbstverständlich auch das wilhelminische *Embellissement* mit seinen ornamentalen Orgien als Maskerade eines sozialpolitischen Skandals begriffen. Den Kodex für diese Sichtweise schuf Werner Hegemann mit seinem Buch „Das steinerne Berlin" (1930). Er entlarvte den Bodenwucher und die Bourgeoisie als die Mächte des Unheils. Hegemann artikulierte das große Motiv, das fünfzehn Jahre später seine Gewalt entfalten sollte: Wahre, das heißt soziale Stadtplanung allein konnte vom „deutschen Wahn" erlösen. Die Gartenstadt, die er für das Volk forderte, sei der Garant für eine Friedenspolitik. Derart begann die Hegemonie der Sozialpolitik in Berlin, die auch die Stadtplanung unterwarf.

So stand Berlin nach 1945 im Banne radikaler Utopien, die sich zu einem einzigen Sprengsatz mischten: die Flucht vor der nationalsozialistischen Vergangenheit in die neue Gesellschaft, der funktionalistische Traum von der modernen Metropole, der sozialhygienische Furor, der die Stunde für eine Kausalbehandlung gekommen sah. Hinzu kam die

and West Berlin. In West Berlin the state even subsidised the removal of stuccos, caryatids and cherubs which originated from the Wilhelminian era. This purification mania was brought to notice in Wolf Jobst Siedler's polemic "The murdered city" (Die gemordete Stadt, 1961). The way in which the SPD and SED viewed the city was dominated by dark inner courtyards and not by the outward facing wall with its beautiful façades. These parties could now advance on the city of class-based misery. As antagonistic as they were towards each other, they shared a vision of the new modern city. At last what had been only imagined in the years before the Second World War was now possible: to get out of the "stony Berlin", to get "out of the grey city walls," as the members of the "free youth movement" sang in the Weimar era.

Capital of the GDR. *In East Berlin, all the utopias of city destruction had to also pay heed to the concept of the "capital of the GDR". In 1950, the city palace of the Hohenzollern dynasty was torn down – to make way for the central speaker's platform and the military parade ground. Both cut across the spatial link between medieval city and baroque city extension. The Bauakademie, Schinkel's last work, which became the model for northern European administrative buildings, was razed in order to provide space for the foreign ministry. The whole of old Berlin between Alexanderplatz and the palace was sacrificed in order to realise the utopian idyll of broad flowing urban spaces in the city centre. Space was a free luxury. "The land had no value," explained the last East Berlin city planning director following the fall of the Wall. Thus there emerged lawn spaces, traffic spaces, dirt spaces, in short: public spaces without a public. The spaces had "lost the power to assemble, that is, to separate and to connect" (Hannah Arendt). They were dominated by powerful gusts and now and then a mass demonstration.*

Asocial centre. *The emptied centre was no longer linked, but separated. The contourless draughty dimensionlessness of the spaces no longer allowed for civil dimensions. But there were also less dramatic but nevertheless enduring processes of decay. The car-friendly curving traffic arteries ruined the rational angular geometry of the baroque and created a city of blunt angles. Dictated by the need for light, air and sun, the apartment blocks were angled away from the street line and positioned behind grass barriers. Since the small plot as a form of property and thus small-scale structuring of urban space also vanished, only the large grid, the placement of buildings and the layout of apartments counted. The concept of the façade lost its meaning, and the architectural repertoire was vulgarised. The result was the monotony of "vulgar modernity" (Siedler). Berlin was struck by an epidemic of formal impoverishment and deformation. Zones of invisibility developed, with entire parts of the city no longer leaving a trace in the inner eye of the inhabitant.*

The violence of the social utopia also deformed the social structure of the city. A city emerged in which eighty per cent of the

verkehrstechnische Utopie der modernen Stadt, die allen das Recht auf frei fließenden Verkehr garantiert. Geschichtsvergessenheit war das gemeinsame Band. Die Verkehrsplanung und der soziale Wohnungsbau konnten mit der Enteignungswut des Staates rechnen. Weder Grundbesitz noch das Stadtbild konnten die neue Stadt aufhalten. Die antiurbanen Funktionsutopien eines Le Corbusier mit seinem *Plan Voisin* (1925) oder eines Ludwig Hilberseimer mit seiner *City-Bebauung* (1927) hatten zum ersten Mal in der Geschichte Platz. Es ist eine viel zu wenig beachtete Tatsache: Nach 1945 blieben nur noch die Arbeiterparteien als gestaltende Kräfte übrig; sie regierten im Osten und im Westen Berlins. Der Staat subventionierte in West-Berlin sogar das Abschlagen des Stucks, der Atlanten, der Karyatiden und Putten, welche die wilhelminische Stadt aufgetragen hatte. Dieser Reinigungswahn wurde erst durch Wolf Jobst Siedlers Streitschrift „Die gemordete Stadt“ (1961) bewußt. Die Stadtoptik von SPD und SED war vom lichtlosen Hinterhof geprägt und nicht von der Straßenseite mit ihren schönen Fassaden. Diese Parteien konnten nun gegen die Stadt des Klassenelends vorrücken. So verfeindet sie auch waren, so einig waren sie sich in der Konkurrenz um die neue moderne Stadt. Endlich war es möglich, was in den Jahren vor dem Zweiten Weltkrieg erträumt wurde: das Heraus aus dem „steinernen Berlin“, das Heraus „aus grauer Städte Mauern“, wie die bündische Jugend der Weimarer Zeit sang.

Hauptstadt der DDR. Zu allen Utopien der Stadtzerstörung kamen in Ost-Berlin die Belange der „Hauptstadt der DDR“ hinzu. Das Stadtschloß der Hohenzollern wurde 1950 abgerissen – für die zentrale Rednertribüne und den Aufmarschplatz. Beides zerschnitt das städtebauliche Gelenk zwischen mittelalterlicher Stadt und barocker Stadterweiterung. Die Bauakademie, Schinkels letztes Werk, das zum Modell für die Amtsbauten Nordeuropas werden sollte, wurde geschleift, um der riesigen Scheibe des Außenministeri-

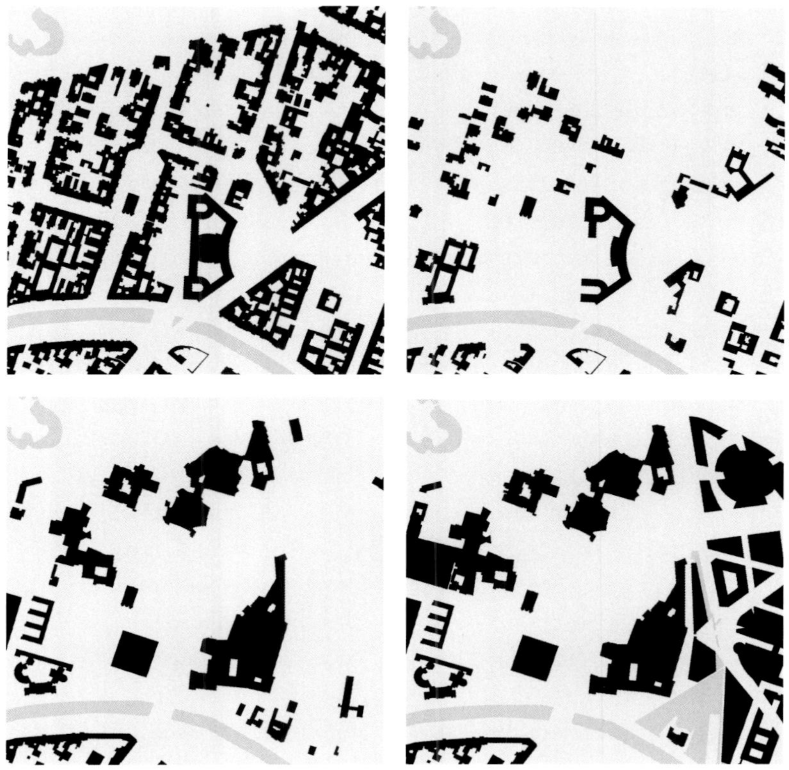

Das Areal des heutigen Kulturforums 1940, 1953, 1989, 2000
The site of the present-day Kulturforum 1940, 1953, 1989, 2000

inhabitants were renters, a phenomenon unique in Europe. The classical street ensemble of the metropolis was undermined. The passer-by, the flâneur, the market crier, all representatives of everyday urban interaction, disappeared. The figure of the citoyen, the city burgher who felt responsible for the demands of the community, was regarded as obsolete. The inhabitant dominated. He announced his egalitarian claim to affordable housing, good transport connections and a certain percentage of greenery, and evaded all obligations in regard to the city. Civil society was transformed into sociology. Social policy was desocialised, the individual stripped of his citizenship.

The view of the Wall. *Of course there were also counter-currents from the 1970s onwards, as there were in other West German cities. The squatters in West Berlin defended the social diversity, the variety and wealth of city images of popular quarters in Kreuzberg and in Wedding. Settlements which extended over several blocks were stopped and strategies to preserve small-scale social units were developed. But the social and historical unit of reference was always the "Kiez", the quarter, never the entire city. Kiez bigotry was also a consequence of the Wall. It divided not only Berlin but also undermined the idea of the city as a whole. In the course of the years it retrospectively extinguished the history of the city. The historical centre became a district of East Berlin, bereft of aura, authority and historical claim.*

The Wall not only divided the people, but also Berlin from the Berliners. It deformed the view of one's own city; it sabotaged the perception of the creeping loss of urban substance. The knowledge of one's own city and the consciousness of the city image, of the form of the urban environment and the context of the streets was eroded. In the schools, the history of the city was no longer taught, only the history of city districts.

The fall of the Wall has also meant the collapse of the constellation of factors impeding the gaze. It is the moment of truth. But the eye must first readjust itself. It must learn to see what is documented in the harsh X-ray light of the black plans. The evi-

ums Platz zu machen. Ganz Alt-Berlin zwischen Alexanderplatz und Schloß wurde geopfert, um jene utopischen Idyllen der weiten fließenden Stadträume im Zentrum Wirklichkeit werden zu lassen. Raum war kostenloser Luxus. „Der Grund und Boden hatte ja keinen Wert", erklärte der letzte Ost-Berliner Stadtplaner nach der Wende. So entstanden Rasenräume, Verkehrsräume, Schmuddelräume, kurz: öffentliche Räume ohne Öffentlichkeit. Die Räume hatten die „Kraft verloren, zu versammeln, das heißt zu trennen und zu verbinden" (Hannah Arendt). Was da herrschte, das war die Zugluft und dann und wann eine Massendemonstration.

Asoziale Mitte. Das entleerte Zentrum verband nicht mehr, es trennte. Die konturlose zugige Maßstabslosigkeit der Räume erlaubte keine zivilen Maßstäbe mehr. Aber es gab auch weniger dramatische und dennoch nachhaltige Zerfallsprozesse. Die autofreundlichen geschwungenen Verkehrsadern ruinierten die rationale Winkelgeometrie des Barock und schufen eine Stadt der stumpfen Winkel. Unter dem Diktat von Licht, Luft und Sonne wurden die Wohnblocks aus der Straßenflucht weggedreht und in Abstandsgrün gebettet. Da auch die Parzelle als Eigentumsform und damit die Kleinteiligkeit verschwand, zählte nur noch der große Raster, die Anordnung der Baukörper und der Wohnungsschnitt. Das Thema Fassade verlor seine Bedeutung, und das Repertoire des Architekten vulgarisierte. Das Ergebnis war die Monotonie der „Vulgärmoderne" (Siedler). Eine Epidemie der Gestaltarmut und Ent-Gestaltung überzog Berlin. Es entstanden Zonen der Unsichtbarkeit. Ganze Teile der Stadt hinterlassen keine Spur mehr im inneren Auge des Städters.

Die Gewalt der sozialen Utopie deformierte auch das soziale Gebilde Stadt. Es entstand das europäische Unikum einer achtzigprozentigen Mieterstadt. Das klassische Straßen-Ensemble der Metropole wurde ausgedünnt. Der Passant, der Flaneur, der Marktschreier, der Volkstribun auf dem Platz, sie alle die Repräsentanten des alltäglichen Stadtgesprächs, verschwanden. Die Figur des Citoyen, des Stadtbürgers, der sich für die Belange des Gemeinwesens verantwortlich fühlt, galt als obsolet. Der Einwohner dominierte. Er meldete seinen egalitären Anspruch auf preiswerten Wohnraum, guter Verkehrsanbindung und einen Prozentsatz an Stadtgrün an und entzog sich allen Pflichten gegenüber der Stadt. Die Zivilgesellschaft verwandelte sich in Soziologie. Die Sozialpolitik entsozialisierte, entkleidete den Menschen seiner Stadtbürgerschaft.

Die Optik der Mauer. Natürlich gab es auch Gegenbewegungen seit den 70er Jahren, wie in anderen westdeutschen Städten auch. Die Hausbesetzer in West-Berlin verteidigten die soziale Vielfalt, die Mischung und den Stadtbildreichtum der volkstümlichen Quartiere in Kreuzberg und Wedding.

dence must be exposed under the sedimentary layers of utopias. For what has been described as the destruction of the city has also been, as we have seen, the history of enormous efforts to create new city images. It is painful to correct the utopian deformation of one's own eye, especially when this deformation has rested on so much good will. But the end result is shameful and brutal: like no other city in the world, Berlin, as a city of modernity, illustrates the triumph and tragedy of modernity. Berlin as a city of the welfare state demonstrates just as harshly the extent to which the social behaviour of the citizen can be destroyed.

Modern architecture did not do itself any favours when it aimed to base its formal freedom on a tabula rasa. *By doing this it also eliminated the confrontation with the concrete resistance of the historical city. It assumed a responsibility beyond its own capacity and this led to its failure. Fifty years of effort devoted to the new city have not created a single place which draws people to it, which radiates an urban "obligation to encounter" (Hoffmann-Axthelm). The fact that people have voted with their feet is unambiguous: everywhere in the city centre where the utopias of light-air-sun residential buildings have been realised and where the large traffic and green spaces dominate, the current of passers-by has dried up. They are dead zones.*

Hic salta. *But what is to be the point of reference if something new is to emerge? Does this mean that the barbaric acts of the liquidation of history since 1945 should in turn be liquidated with the same energy? What is to be done with the history of the city that in part slumbers under the asphalt of parking lots and continues to live in the layout of the city structure? This decision applies to the entire historical centre. As in the states of central-eastern Europe, the post-utopian era has begun in Berlin as well. And like Germany, Berlin has won back its sovereignty. Where then lies the foundation of the future? Should Berlin draw a line under what is past and commit the future of the city to the fashions of modernity? Or should Berlin examine its historical substance, critically reconstruct its disappearance and finally struggle for a genuine compromise between city history and modernity? Whatever the decision, it is a decision which will be final. Berlin stands before this caesura – it is a decision which will shape architectural history. Anyone who does not commit themselves to Schinkel's Bauakademie, which lives on in the minds of Berliners, will definitely obliterate it.*

The Piranesian transition. *The transition which Berlin faces is also a transition in terms of viewpoint. We must look again at what is present of the historical. We are invited to participate in a paradoxical exercise of decoding the visible, to adopt a method associated with such renowned protagonists as Giovanni Battista Piranesi. In the* antichità romane *he dug out from the layer of the everyday perception of a rurally neglected Rome the grandeur of imperial urbanity. From the contemporary* campo vacchi, *the pasture, the forum romanum. A photograph-*

Die blockübergreifenden Sozialsiedlungen wurden gestoppt und Strategien der Rettung entwickelt. Aber die soziale und historische Bezugsgröße war immer der „Kiez“, das Viertel, nie die Gesamtstadt. Kiezborniertheit war auch eine der Mauerfolgen. Sie teilte nicht nur Berlin, sondern zersetzte auch die Vorstellung von der Gesamtstadt. Im Lauf der Jahre löschte sie rückwirkend die Stadtgeschichte. Das historische Zentrum verwandelte sich in einen Ost-Berliner Stadtteil, ohne Ausstrahlung, ohne Autorität und ohne geschichtlichen Anspruch.

Die Mauer trennte nicht nur die Menschen, sondern auch Berlin von den Berlinern. Sie deformierte die Optik, die Sicht auf die eigene Stadt; sie sabotierte die Wahrnehmung des schleichenden Verlustes von urbaner Substanz. Das Wissen über die eigene Stadt wie auch das Bewußtsein von einem Stadtbild, von der Stadtgestalt und dem Kontext der Straßen erodierte. An den Schulen wurde nicht mehr Stadtgeschichte, sondern nur nach Stadtteilgeschichte gelehrt.

Mit dem Fall der Mauer ist auch der Verblendungszusammenhang gefallen. Es ist die Stunde der Wahrheit. Aber das Auge muß sich erst umstellen. Es muß sehen lernen, was im harten Röntgenlicht der Schwarzpläne dokumentiert wird. Die Evidenz gilt es von den Sedimentschichten der Utopien freizulegen. Denn was als Stadtzerstörung beschrieben wird, war eben auch, wie wir sahen, die Geschichte ungeheurer Anstrengungen, neue Stadtbilder zu schaffen. Es tut weh, die utopische Deformation des eigenen Auges zu korrigieren, zumal wenn sie auf so viel gutem Willen beruhte. Aber die Bilanz ist beschämend und brutal: Berlin, als Stadt der Moderne, zeigt wie keine andere Stadt sonst in der Welt Triumph und Tragik der Moderne. Berlin, als Stadt des Sozialstaates, demonstriert ebenso hart, wie tiefgreifend das stadtbürgerliche Sozialverhalten zerstört werden kann.

Die moderne Architektur hat sich keinen Gefallen getan, als sie ihre Gestaltungsfreiheit auf eine *tabula rasa* gründen wollte. Sie hat sich damit auch der Auseinandersetzung mit dem Realwiderstand der historischen Stadt entledigt. Sie hat eine Verantwortung übernommen, die alle Kräfte überstieg und sie scheitern ließ. Fünfzig Jahre Anstrengung um die neue Stadt haben nicht einen einzigen Platz geschaffen, der die Menschen anzieht, der eine urbane „Begegnungspflicht“ (Hoffmann-Axthelm) ausstrahlt. Die Abstimmung mit den Füßen ist eindeutig: Überall dort, wo im Zentrum die Utopien der Lichtluftsonne-Wohnhäuser verwirklicht wurden und wo die großen Verkehrs- und Grünräume herrschen, versiegt der Strom der Passanten. Es sind tote Zonen.

Hic salta. Aber woran anknüpfen, wenn Neues entstehen soll? Heißt das, die barbarischen Akte der Geschichtsliquidation seit 1945 mit der gleichen Energie wieder liquidieren? Was tun mit der Stadtgeschichte, die zum Teil unerlöst unter

ic report in the Rome of Clemens XIII would also have depicted a very lively city of the fragmentary and the improvisational, with taverns between acanthus capitals and workshops in columned halls. The transition made by Piranesi consists in tipping over the evidence of the present, of representing that which is contemporary as merely a silhouette upon the ruins and bringing forth the topicality of history. This has nothing to do with nostalgia. The modernity of Piranesi still has an effect today. His work of mannered melancholy deals with the presence of the past, from which the future arises.

Although Berlin is a young city, this does not necessarily preclude the association with Piranesi. The antichità berlinese *also imposes this melancholy exertion of the reconstructing imagination in order to free its historical depth from the Brandenburgian sand. The aim of the Piranesian transition is: return, healing, reconciliation. This is by no means an intellectual programme and certainly not an antithesis: the transition to a state of healing arises from the concrete energies of the city which have been liberated by the fall of the Wall. For this is the miracle: although the totalitarian furore of modern utopias was able to play itself out to the very limit in Berlin, the city is now revealing its indestructability. It avenges itself with retreat or dilapidation as long as the urban planning occupation continues. But as soon as the* genius loci *are sought under the foundations of the Wall, it emerges and begins to live. The city's memory is stronger than any programme of historical liquidation. Magic produces not only the fragment and the fire wall, but also the* antichità berlinese. *Oranienburger Strasse, which was a site of street prostitution before the building of the Wall, briefly returned to its old function following the fall of the Wall. The prostitutes went to work, and they were by no means experts in the field of city history.*

V. Paradoxical identity and healing

Berlin antinomy. *Berlin's reputation among the architects of the world is a dubious one. However, intimate knowledge and historico-theoretical exertion is needed to understand the city and to decode the complicated content of magic and fragment, of utopia and destruction. Berlin must be defended against the common and cheap accusation that it is merely timid, antimodern and nostalgic – not for the sake of the city, but because of the insight that is offered here. This aspersion dates back to the so-called "Berlin architectural dispute" of 1992 and the conflict between investors and building authorities. The latter subjected architectural activity to urban development regulations which included, for example, maintaining the historical height of eaves, stone façades and the traditional structure of plots. Such an approach was seen as historically regressive. The Berlin dogmas clashed against one another. The modernity camp armed itself with the*

dem Asphalt der Parkplätze dämmert und im Muster der Stadtstruktur weiterlebt? Diese Entscheidungssituation gilt für das ganze historische Zentrum. Auch in Berlin hat wie in den Staaten Mittelosteuropas das nachutopische Zeitalter begonnen. Und wie Deutschland hat Berlin seine Souveränität wiedererlangt. Wo liegt nun das Fundament der Zukunft? Soll Berlin einen Schlußstrich ziehen und die Zukunft der Stadt den Moden der Moderne anheimgeben? Oder soll Berlin die geschichtliche Substanz überprüfen, ihre Löschungen kritisch rekonstruieren und nun endlich um einen wirklichen Kompromiß zwischen Stadtgeschichte und Moderne ringen? Wie auch immer entschieden wird – nunmehr ist die Entscheidung endgültig. Vor dieser Zäsur steht Berlin – es ist eine Entscheidungssituation, die die Architekturgeschichte prägen wird. Wer sich jetzt nicht für Schinkels Bauakademie engagiert, die noch immer in den Köpfen der Berliner fortlebt, wird sie definitiv auslöschen.

Die Piranesische Wende. Diese Wende, vor der Berlin steht, heißt auch Blickwende. Es gilt, neu zu sehen, was an alter Geschichte gegenwärtig ist. Eingeladen wird zu einer paradoxen Übung der Entzifferung des Sichtbaren, zu einer Methode, die so grandiose Protagonisten kennt wie Giovanni Battista Piranesi. In den *Antichità Romane* grub er aus der Schicht alltäglicher Wahrnehmung eines ländlich verwahrlosten Roms die Grandeur imperialer Urbanität. Er schuf aus dem zeitgenössischen *campo vacchi*, der Kuhweide, das Forum romanum. Eine Photoreportage im Rom von Clemens XIII. hätte auch eine höchst lebendige Stadt des Fragments und der Improvisation abgebildet, mit Osterien zwischen Akanthuskapitellen und Werkstätten in Säulenhallen. Die Wende von Piranesi besteht darin, die Evidenz der Gegenwart zu kippen, die reale Zeitgenossenschaft nur noch als Schemen auf den Ruinenabgründen darzustellen und die Aktualität der Geschichte hervorzuholen. Das hat nichts mit Nostalgie zu tun. Die Modernität Piranesis wirkt bis heute. Sein Werk manieristischer Melancholie arbeitet mit der Gegenwart der Vergangenheit, aus der die Zukunft entsteht.

Obwohl Berlin eine junge Stadt ist, muß die Assoziation Piranesi nicht unstatthaft sein. Auch die *Antichità berlinese* nötigen uns diese melancholische Anspannung der rekonstruierenden Phantasie auf, um ihre historische Tiefe aus dem märkischen Sand zu befreien. Das Ziel der Piranesischen Wende ist: Wiederkehr, Heilung, Versöhnung. Das ist keineswegs ein intellektuelles Programm und schon gar nicht eine Antithese: Die Wende zur Heilung entspringt den realen Kräften der Stadt, die durch den Fall der Mauer befreit wurden. Denn das ist das Wunder: Obwohl sich in Berlin der totalitäre Furor moderner Utopien bis zur letzten Konsequenz austoben konnte, zeigt jetzt die Stadt ihre Unzerstörbarkeit. Sie rächt sich mit Rückzug oder Verwahrlosung,

sentence by Karl Scheffler, according to which Berlin "is damned to forever be in the process of becoming but never to be." The urban planning camp countered with the assertion that "Berlin is and does not first have to be invented." It was a pointless debate, which postulated as truths what could only become true through a process of self-reflection. Faced with an initial speculative mania, the building authorities had to anticipate a Berlin identity which a slowly awakening urban society was just beginning to appreciate.

Marienkirche and Fernsehturm. *The dogma dispute is merely the ideological reflex of a unique urban planning and political situation. There is no metropolitan city in the world in which the historical centre must first be reconstructed. The commitment of the global architectural scene and the flood of designs since 1989 clearly show that more is at stake than merely the closing of existing gaps and intermediate spaces. It concerns the great challenge of resolving Berlin's East-West conflict. The development of the city centre is faced with the demand of winning back or creating a city image. But from where should this come?*

The touchiness and ideological doggedness characterising the worldwide architectural debate on Berlin arises from the suspicion that the challenges of the city will make the crisis of modernity more acute. This is ultimately why what remains of GDR modernism, which prior to the fall of the Wall was regarded as the epigonic rearguard of the prevailing architectural fashions, is defended. The urban developmental writing of Berlin is not a coherent, convincing text. The most extreme example is the historical centre itself: the giant GDR buildings stand there in a state of chronic hostility towards their surroundings. The Palast der Republik destroys the dimensions of the ensemble of Zeughaus, Museumsinsel and Cathedral. It pushes its way at an angle to the site of the city palace into the axis of Unter den Linden. The Staatratsgebäude destroys Brüderstrasse. These collisions can increase to the limits of aesthetic acceptability: St Marien, the oldest of Berlin's churches and the church of the citizenry sits in a hollow as if it were slowly sinking. It practically disappears in the grey shaft of the Fernsehturm (the television tower) the height of which ridicules the Gothic symbol. The enormous substructures of the tower reach for the church like paws. Around it stretches a huge formless square upon which the major part of medieval Berlin once stood. This square, the birthplace of the city, does not even have a name. In the middle of Berlin's centre, one encounters cannibalism.

The present condition of the centre in itself already pushes towards revision. In Berlin the issue is nothing less than the complicated operation of restoring urban developmental normality. For the future of cities has always come from the past, arising from their continuity or from the particular negation of it. The goal is not nostalgia or historical mimicry. The brutal contrast of St Marien and the Fernsehturm cannot be undone. But the

solange die stadtplanerischen Okkupationen anhalten. Sobald aber der *genius loci* gesucht wird unter den Fundamenten der Mauer, taucht er auf und beginnt zu leben. Das Gedächtnis der Stadt ist stärker als alle Geschichtslöschungsprogramme. Magie produzieren nicht nur Fragment und Brandmauer, sondern auch die *Antichità berlinese*. Die Oranienburger Straße, vor dem Mauerbau der Ort der Straßenprostitution, kehrte augenblicklich nach dem Fall der Mauer zu ihrer alten städtischen Funktion zurück, die Huren nahmen ihre Arbeit auf, und sie waren keineswegs Expertinnen der Stadtgeschichte.

V. Paradoxe Identität und Heilung

Berliner Antinomie. Berlins Ruf unter den Architekten der Welt ist fragwürdig. Aber es bedarf auch intimer Kenntnis und geschichtstheoretischer Anstrengung, um die Stadt zu verstehen und um den komplizierten Sachverhalt von Magie und Fragment, von Utopie und Zerstörung zu entschlüsseln. Berlin muß gegen den üblichen und wohlfeilen Vorwurf verteidigt werden, es sei nur ängstlich, antimodern und nostalgisch – nicht um der Stadt willen, sondern der Erkenntnis wegen, die hier angeboten wird. Diese Fama nahm ihren Anfang mit dem sogenannten „Berliner Architekturstreit" von 1992 und dem Konflikt zwischen Investoren und Bauverwaltung. Diese erlegte den Architekten städtebauliche Regeln auf, die Verpflichtung auf die historische Traufhöhe, die Blockrandbebauung, die steinernen Fassaden und die traditionelle Parzellenstruktur. Ein solcher Ansatz galt als historistischer Rückfall. Die Berlindogmen prallten aufeinander. Die Moderne bewaffnete sich mit dem Satz von Karl Scheffler, wonach Berlin dazu „verdammt ist, immerfort zu werden und niemals zu sein". Die Stadtplanung setzte dagegen, daß „Berlin ist und nicht erst erfunden werden muß". Es war eine aussichtslose Debatte, die als Wahrheiten postulierte, was erst durch einen Selbstbesinnungsprozeß wahr werden konnte. Die Bauverwaltung mußte gegen die Spekulationswut der ersten Stunde eine Berliner Identität antizipieren, die eine langsam zu sich kommende Stadtgesellschaft gerade erst zu ertasten begann.

Marienkirche und Fernsehturm. Der Dogmenstreit ist nur der ideologische Reflex einer einzigartigen stadtplanerischen und stadtpolitischen Situation. Es gibt keine Metropole in der Welt, in der das historische Zentrum erst wieder rekonstruiert werden muß. Das Engagement der globalen Architekturszene und die Flut von Entwurfsvisionen seit 1989 zeigen deutlich, daß mehr auf dem Spiel steht als nur das Schließen vorhandener Lücken und Zwischenräume. Es geht um die große Herausforderung, den Ost-West-Gegensatz Berlins zu versöhnen. Und noch um etwas mehr: Die Bebau-

church has a claim to an appropriate structural environment, to the recreation of the historical Marienkirchhof, which would, for example, separate it from the obscene effect of the adjacent concrete mass.

The miracle of return. *Patience is necessary to arrive at imaginative compromises and aesthetic precision. Such things do not emerge on the drawing-boards of architects or the desks of planners. Here, the inhabitants must play a part, here the population's sensibility for the city image must emerge. And it is already stirring: quarters and streets are awakening, discovering their old significance and interpreting it anew. An example is the Spandauer Vorstadt on the edge of the centre: here the young generation of unified Berlin has forced its way into history and has arrived in the future. The district exhibits the glow of urban intelligence and service-sector competition, of luxury, refinement and fashion – a place between the Internet and old Berlin. Seventy galleries, numerous restaurants serving fashionable cuisine, studios, design centres, agencies and directors of nightlife operate here. The names of establishments combine intellectual allusions with newly discovered tradition. Here tradition is being reinvented. Around the synagogue in Oranienburger Strasse a scene made up of kosher cultural centres, shops and Jewish cultural institutions is emerging – a new Jewish quarter – the return of which is as surprising and self-evident as the reconstruction of the city's centre will be. A new intellectual culture is developing, shaped by nervousness, scepticism, curiosity and narcissism, which knows how to make use of the driving force of the* genius loci. *The cult of anomaly and the fragment no longer has a place there.*

It is a mass movement of individuals: in 1989 the Berliners began to walk through the cityscape of the centre and to renew the memory of the city. Exemplary here are the debates over the reconstruction of the city palace. Since the Hamburg merchant Wilhelm von Boddin had a painted façade erected on the former site of the palace and first made its loss visible, the building designed by Schlüter has been growing into reality. At first the East-West dispute raged. The Palast der Republik faced the Hohenzollern cult, with the architectural dispute between modernity and historical revisionism also playing a part. However, the fronts are gradually becoming less rigid, ideas are piling up and the ideologies are fading because they are ultimately boring. The real theme is coming to the fore: the beauty of the city. Beauty means the recovery of a city image, of an ensemble between the Lustgarten and Schlossplatz, the dimensions and internal order of which referred to the palace. Beauty heals; it is the sought after third element, the internal image of identity in which East and West can become reconciled. This insight is growing in the city.

Manfred Hamm's photographs have appeared at this exciting moment in the history of the city. Their classicism also springs from the Piranesian transition. They reinvent the beauty inher-

ung des Zentrums steht unter dem Anspruch, ein Stadtbild zurückzugewinnen oder zu schaffen. Aber woher soll es kommen?

Die Gereizheit und ideologische Verbissenheit der weltweiten Architekturdebatte über Berlin entspringt der Ahnung, daß die Herausforderungen der Stadt die Krise der Moderne akut werden lassen. Darum wird letztlich auch die Hinterlassenschaft der DDR-Moderne, die vor dem Mauerfall nur als epigonale Nachhut der jeweiligen Architekturmoden galt, summarisch verteidigt. Die städtebauliche Schrift Berlins ergibt keinen zusammenhängenden, überzeugenden Text. Extremstes Beispiel ist das historische Zentrum selbst: Die DDR-Großbauten stehen da in chronischer Feindseligkeit zur Umgebung. Der Palast der Republik destruiert den Maßstab des Ensembles von Zeughaus, Museumsinsel und Dom. Er drängt sich, quer zur Kubatur des Stadtschlosses, in die Lindenachse hinein. Das Staatsratsgebäude zerstört die Brüderstraße. Diese Kollisionen können sich bis zur ästhetischen Schmerzgrenze steigern: St. Marien, die älteste Kirche Berlins und die eigentliche Kirche der Bürgerschaft, steckt in einer Vertiefung, als ob sie langsam versinken würde. Sie verschwindet praktisch in dem grauen Schaft des Fernsehturms, dessen Höhe das gotische Wahrzeichen ridikülisiert. Die riesigen Substrukturen des Turms greifen wie Tatzen nach der Kirche. Darum herum erstreckt sich ein riesiger formloser Platz, auf dem einst der größte Teil des mittelalterlichen Berlins stand. Dieser Platz, der Geburtsort der Stadt, hat nicht einmal einen Namen. Mitten im Berliner Zentrum begegnet man dem architektonischen Kannibalismus.

Schon der gegenwärtige Zustand des Zentrums zwingt zur Revision. In Berlin geht es um nichts weniger als um die komplizierte Operation der Wiederherstellung städtebaulicher Normalität. Denn die Zukunft der Städte kam immer aus der Vergangenheit, entstand aus ihrer Kontinuität oder aus der bestimmten Negation zu ihr. Nicht Nostalgie oder historistische Mimikry ist das Ziel. Der brutale Gegensatz von St. Marien und Fernsehturm läßt sich nicht ungeschehen machen. Aber die Kirche hat einen Anspruch auf eine angemessene bauliche Umgebung, auf Neuschöpfung des historischen Marienkirchhofes, der sie zum Beispiel von dem obszönen Zugriff der Betonmassen nebenan trennt.

Das Wunder der Wiederkehr. Geduld ist vonnöten, um zu phantasievollen Kompromissen und ästhetischer Präzision zu kommen. So etwas entsteht nicht allein an den Reißbrettern der Architekten oder den Schreibtischen der Planer. Hier muß sich der Städter bewegen, muß eine stadtbürgerliche Sensibilität für das Stadtbild entstehen. Und sie regt sich schon: Stadtteile und Straßen erwachen, entdecken ihre alte Bedeutung und interpretieren sie neu. Zum Beispiel ein

ent in Berlin. They are an individual vision and at the same time document the way things stand. The "beauty of the large city" emerges in the eye of the urban inhabitant, in the school of seeing, as August Endell teaches. Manfred Hamm is training the eye of the present day Berliner. His photographs are also a school of seeing; he constructs continuity.

The two attractions with which the "new Berlin" advertises itself symbolise this transition in their own way: the Reichstag dome and the Hackesche Höfe courtyard complex. The Hackesche Höfe draw in people not only because of their unique Art Nouveau beauty. Their small-scale, lively labyrinths and arcades populated by shops, galleries and bistros are a hymn to the vitality and potential of the old city structure. They teach us to live with urban density and to enjoy it. The Hackesche Höfe have initiated the discovery of courtyards as living space. They are urban educational establishments, in which the consumer is re-educated as a flâneur.

The emergence of the Reichstag dome is also a sign. It came out of the climate of ideological suspicion. When, during the conversion of the parliament building, the restoration of the dome was demanded by different members of parliament, there emerged what is known in Germany as Historikerstreit. The dome was seen as a reactionary, even monarchist manifesto, whereas only the flat glass roof, seen as ideologically correct, befitted democracy. The badgered architect Norman Foster produced twenty-six designs for the Reichstag roof, ranging from glass boxes to an egg-shaped form. In the end the transparent dome with its spiral staircase triumphed. It now illuminates the interior, and the dainty shadows of the visitors circle like the workings of a clock above the assembly room. The dome has become the symbol of the Berlin republic and of the strength of urban reconciliation. Now Berlin finally also has a point de vue, *from which it can let itself be seen. In the view from the glass dome, the new reconciliation combines itself with the city image. This process is one of urban self-reflection and emancipation from the ideologies, misgivings and convictions of the post-war period. The vision of success which the dome and the Hackesche Höfe announce was lacking for so long. Now Berlin is coming to its senses, and it is even discovering the democratic optimism which Franz Hessel sensed in the Weimar period. Finally.*

◆

Viertel wie die Spandauer Vorstadt am Rande des Zentrums: Hier ist die junge Generation des vereinten Berlins in die Geschichte eingedrungen und in der Zukunft angekommen. Über dem Viertel liegt der Schimmer von Großstadtintelligenz und Dienstleistungskonkurrenz, von Luxus, Raffinement und Moden – ein Ort zwischen Internet und Alt-Berlin. Siebzig Galerien, unzählige Restaurants mit Trendküche, Hutateliers, Designcenter, Eventagenturen, Regisseure der Nachtschwärmerei agieren da. Die Namen der Etablissements schillern zwischen intellektuellen Anspielungen und frisch entdeckter Tradition. Hier wird die Tradition neu erfunden. Rund um die Synagoge in der Oranienburger Straße entsteht eine Szene mit koscheren Kultureinrichtungen, Läden und jüdischen Kulturinstitutionen, ein neues jüdisches Viertel, dessen Wiederkehr so überraschend und selbstverständlich erscheint, wie es die Rekonstruktion des Zentrums sein wird. Eine neue intellektuelle Kultur entwickelt sich, geprägt von Nervosität, Skepsis, Neugier und Narzißmus, die die Triebkraft des *genius loci* zu nutzen weiß. Der Kult der Anomalie und des Fragments hat da keinen Platz mehr.

Es ist eine Massenbewegung von Einzelnen: 1989 haben die Berliner begonnen, die Stadtlandschaft des Zentrums zu erwandern und das Gedächtnis der Stadt zu erneuern. Beispielhaft sind die Debatten über die Rekonstruktion des Stadtschlosses. Seitdem der Hamburger Kaufmann Wilhelm von Boddien 1993 die gemalte Fassade in der Kubatur des Schlosses vor Augen gestellt und den Verlust überhaupt erst sichtbar gemacht hatte, wächst der Schlüterbau in die Wirklichkeit hinein. Zunächst tobte der Ost-West-Streit. Der Palast der Republik stand gegen Hohenzollernkult. Der Architekturstreit zwischen Moderne und Geschichtsrevisionismus spielte hinein. Aber allmählich werden die Fronten unübersichtlicher, die Ideen häufen sich und die Ideologien verblassen, weil sie letztlich langweilen. Das wirkliche Thema rückt in den Vordergrund: die Schönheit der Stadt. Schönheit heißt hier Wiedergewinnung eines Stadtbildes, eines Ensembles zwischen Lustgarten und Schloßplatz, dessen Maßstäbe und innere Ordnung auf das Schloß bezogen waren. Schönheit heilt, ist das gesuchte Dritte, das innere Bild der Identität, in dem sich Ost und West finden können. Diese Einsicht wächst in der Stadt.

Manfred Hamms Photographien erscheinen in diesem erregenden Moment der Stadtgeschichte. Ihre Klassizität entspringt auch der Piranesischen Wende. Sie erfinden die Berlin innewohnende Schönheit neu. Sie sind eine individuelle Vision und dokumentieren doch zugleich den Stand der Dinge. Die „Schönheit der großen Stadt" entsteht im Auge des Städters, in der Schule des Sehens, lehrte August Endell. Manfred Hamm trainiert das Auge des heutigen Berliners. Auch seine Photographien sind eine Schule des Sehens, er konstruiert Kontinuität.

Jene zwei Attraktionen, mit denen das „neue Berlin" wirbt, symbolisieren auf ihre Art diese Wende: die Reichstagskuppel und die Hackeschen Höfe. Die Hackeschen Höfe ziehen die Menschen nicht nur wegen ihrer einzigartigen Jugendstilschönheit an. Ihre kleinteiligen, lebendigen Labyrinthe und Passagen mit den Läden, Galerien und Bistros sind eine einzige Hymne auf die Vitalität und das Potential der alten Stadtstruktur. Sie lehren, mit der urbanen Dichte zu leben und sie zu genießen. Die Hackeschen Höfe haben die Entdeckung der Höfe als Lebensraum eingeleitet. Es sind städtische Lehranstalten, in denen der Konsument zum Flaneur umgeschult wird.

Auch die Entstehung der Reichtagskuppel ist ein Zeichen. Sie kam aus dem Klima des ideologischen Verdachts. Als bei dem Umbau des Parlamentsgebäudes von verschiedenen Abgeordneten die Wiederherstellung der Kuppel gefordert wurde, begann das, was in Deutschland Historikerstreit heißt. Die Kuppel galt als reaktionäres oder gar monarchistisches Manifest, während das gläserne Flachdach, so wollte es die ideologische Korrektheit, allein der Demokratie gebühre. Der bedrängte Architekt Norman Foster entwarf sechsundzwanzig verschiedene Reichstagsaufsätze, vom gläsernen Kasten bis zum angeschnittenen Ei. Am Ende siegte die durchsichtige Kuppel mit der begehbaren Spirale. Nun leuchtet sie, und die zierlichen Schatten der Besucher kreisen wie in einem Uhrwerk über dem Plenarsaal. Die Kuppel ist zum Wahrzeichen der Berliner Republik geworden und ein Symbol urbaner Versöhnungskraft. Nun hat auch Berlin endlich einen *point de vue*, von dem aus es sich sehen lassen kann. Im Blick aus der gläsernen Halbkugel setzt sich das neue Einverständnis mit dem Stadtbild zusammen. Dieser Prozeß heißt: urbane Selbstbesinnung und Emanzipation von Ideologien, Bedenken und Überzeugungen der Nachkriegsjahrzehnte. Die Vision des Gelingens, die die Kuppel und die Hackeschen Höfe verkünden, wurde so lange entbehrt. Nun kommt Berlin zu sich selbst. Und entdeckt vielleicht sogar den demokratischen Stadtfrohsinn, den Franz Hessel in der Weimarer Zeit spürte. Endlich.

◆

Blick vom Dach des Lindencorsos in Richtung Tiergarten
View from the roof of the Lindencorso looking towards the Tiergarten

Blick vom Dach der Debis-Zentrale am Potsdamer Platz auf die Kuppel des Imax-Kinos, das Sony Center und das Büro- und Geschäftshaus von Hans Kollhoff

View from the roof of the Debis head office at Potsdamer Platz, with the dome of the Imax cinema, the Sony Center and the office and commercial building designed by Hans Kollhoff

Die Quadriga auf dem Brandenburger Tor, im Hintergrund der Potsdamer Platz
The quadriga crowning the Brandenburg Gate with Potsdamer Platz in the background

Reichstagsgebäude mit der Glaskuppel von Sir Norman Foster
The Reichstag building, seat of the German parliament, with the glass dome designed by Sir Norman Foster

Reichstag, Osteingang zum Plenarsaal
The Reichstag building, eastern entrance to the plenary chamber

Blick vom Dach des Lindencorsos Unter den Linden auf Humboldt-Universität, Neue Wache, Zeughaus und Berliner Dom

Unter den Linden seen from the roof of the Lindencorso with the Humboldt University, the Neue Wache (New Guardhouse), the Zeughaus (Arsenal) and Berlin Cathedral

Blick vom Westin Grand Hotel auf die Friedrichstraße

View of Friedrichstrasse from the Westin Grand Hotel

Blick von der Staatsbibliothek Unter den Linden auf den Berliner Dom und den Fernsehturm am Alexanderplatz
View of Berlin Cathedral and the television tower at Alexanderplatz, seen from the State Library on Unter den Linden

Blick von der Berliner Niederlassung der Allianz-Versicherung, Treptow, in Richtung Oberbaumbrücke und Mitte
View of the Oberbaum Bridge and Berlin-Mitte, seen from the Allianz insurance company building in Treptow

Kuppelhalle im Bode-Museum auf der Museumsinsel
The domed hall at the Bode Museum on Museum Island

Nördlicher Abschluß der Museumsinsel mit Bodemuseum und Pergamonmuseum
The north end of Museum Island with the Bode Museum and the Pergamon Museum

Blick von der Debis-Zentrale in Richtung Norden, im Vordergrund das Dach der neuen Staatsbibliothek, dahinter die Philharmonie, im Hintergrund das Haus der Kulturen der Welt (ehemals Kongreßhalle)

Looking north from the Debis head office. In the foreground the roof of the new State Library with the Philharmonie to the rear, in the background the Haus der Kulturen der Welt (House of World Cultures, former Congress Hall)

Blick vom Dach des Wissenschaftszentrums Berlin auf die Neue Nationalgalerie, im Hintergrund die neue Staatsbibliothek und der Potsdamer Platz

View of the New National Gallery from the roof of the Berlin Centre of Sciences, with the new State Library and Potsdamer Platz in the background

oben: Der Hamburger Bahnhof in Tiergarten, 1993-96 von Josef Paul Kleihues zum Museum für Gegenwart umgestaltet
unten: Das Bauhaus-Archiv nach einem Entwurf von Walter Gropius am Landwehrkanal in Tiergarten

above: Hamburger Bahnhof in Tiergarten, the old station redesigned as the Museum of the Present by Josef Paul Kleihues
below: The Bauhaus Archive after a design by Walter Gropius, on the Landwehrkanal in Tiergarten

Museum für Post und Kommunikation in der Leipziger Straße, Mitte
Museum for Post and Communications in Leipziger Strasse, Mitte

Treppenaufgang im Inneren des Jüdischen Museums
The main staircase inside the Jewish Museum

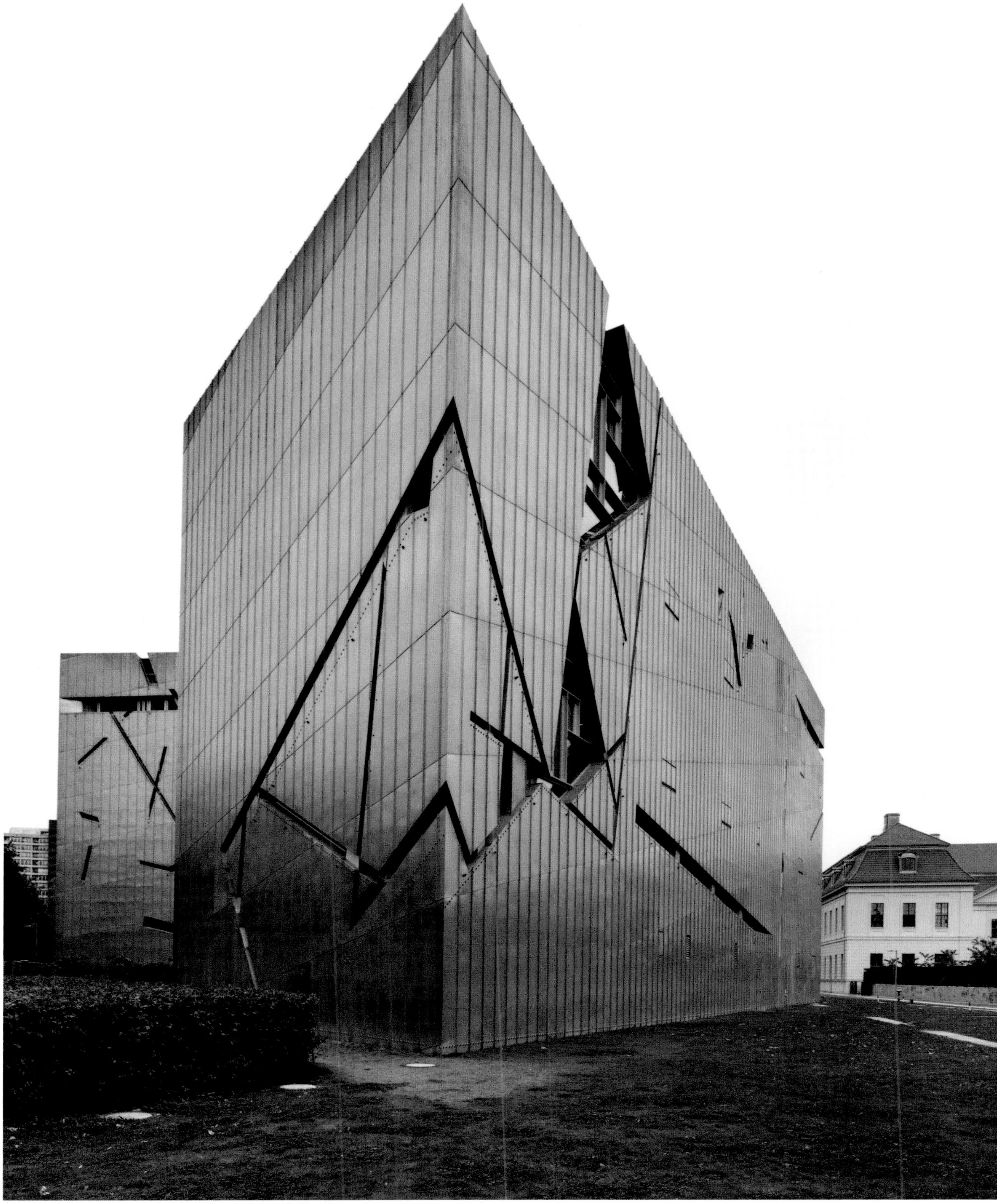

Außenansicht des Jüdischen Museums, Kreuzberg
The Jewish Museum, Kreuzberg

oben: Die Kulturbrauerei, ein Gewerbe- und Kulturzentrum in der ehemaligen Schultheiß-Brauerei, Prenzlauer Berg
unten: Die Skulptur „Houseball“ von Claes Oldenburg in der Mauerstraße, Mitte

above: The Kulturbrauerei, a trade and cultural centre at the former Schultheiss brewery, Prenzlauer Berg
below: Claes Oldenburg's sculpture "Houseball" in Mauerstrasse, Mitte

Neue Synagoge in der Oranienburger Straße
The New Synagogue in Oranienburger Strasse

Hackesche Höfe in Mitte, Hof I
The Hackesche Höfe in Mitte, in the first courtyard

Kurfürstendamm, im Hintergrund die Kaiser-Wilhelm-Gedächtniskirche
Kurfürstendamm with the Kaiser Wilhelm Memorial Church in the background

Blick von der Kantstraße auf die Kaiser-Wilhelm-Gedächtniskirche und das Europa-Center
Looking from Kantstrasse towards the Kaiser Wilhelm Memorial Church and the Europa Center

Das Ludwig-Erhard-Haus in der Fasanenstraße in Charlottenburg, Sitz der Industrie- und Handelskammer Berlin und der Berliner Börse
The Ludwig Erhard Haus on Fasanenstrasse, the seat of the Berlin Chamber of Industry and Commerce and the Berlin stock exchange

Löwen-Brücke im Tiergarten mit bei Johann Friedrich August Borsig gegossenen Skulpturen (1838)
The Lion Bridge in Tiergarten with sculptures cast at the Johann Friedrich August Borsig workshops (1838)

Panzernashorn im Zoologischen Garten
An Indian rhinoceros at the Zoological Gardens

Die Figuren der berühmten „Puppenallee“ im Depot der Berlinischen Galerie im Lapidarium, Kreuzberg
The sculptures from the famous Siegesallee, nicknamed "Puppet Parade", at the Berlinische Galerie depot in the Lapidarium, Kreuzberg

Denkmal Alexander von Humboldts von Reinhold Begas vor der Humboldt-Universität, Unter den Linden
The memorial to Alexander von Humboldt by Reinhold Begas in front of the Humboldt University, Unter den Linden

Blick vom Dach der Deutschen Staatsoper Unter den Linden auf den Portikus der St.-Hedwigs-Kathedrale
The entrance to St Hedwig's Cathedral seen from the roof of the Deutsche Staatsoper on Unter den Linden

Eingangsfront des Alten Museums am Lustgarten
The main façade of the Altes Museum (Old Museum) at the Lustgarten

Rotunde im Alten Museum von Karl Friedrich Schinkel
The rotunda in the Altes Museum (Old Museum) by Karl Friedrich Schinkel

Die Neue Wache Unter den Linden von Karl Friedrich Schinkel (1816-18)
The Neue Wache (New Guardhouse) by Karl Friedrich Schinkel (1816-18) on Unter den Linden

oben: Charité, in der ehemaligen Tierarzneischule
unten: Charité, Anatomisches Theater (ehemalige Zootomie), 1789-90 erbaut von Carl Gotthard Langhans

above: The Charité hospital, in the former school of veterinary medicine
below: The anatomical theatre (former zootomy) at the Charité 1789-90, designed by Carl Gotthard Langhans

Staatsbibliothek Unter den Linden, erbaut 1903-14 von Ernst von Ihne, Katalogsaal an der Charlottenstraße
The State Library on Unter den Linden 1903-14, designed by Ernst von Ihne, the catalogue hall on Charlottenstrasse

S-Bahnhof Hackescher Markt in Mitte
Hackescher Markt S-Bahn station in Mitte

Blick vom Dach des ehemaligen Postfuhramts in der Oranienburger Straße auf die Kuppel der Neuen Synagoge und den Fernsehturm am Alexanderplatz

The New Synagogue dome and the television tower at Alexanderplatz, seen from the Postfuhramt roof (old post office coach station) in Oranienburger Strasse

Die Jungfernbrücke über den Spreekanal, die älteste erhaltene Brücke Berlins (errichtet 1798); im Hintergrund das Gebäude der ehemaligen Reichsbank, heute Sitz des Auswärtigen Amtes

The Jungfernbrücke spanning the Spreekanal, Berlin's oldest surviving bridge (built 1798); in the background the building of the former Reichsbank, now the Ministry of Foreign Affairs

Die Schloßbrücke von Karl Friedrich Schinkel (1821-24), im Hintergrund der Berliner Dom und der Fernsehturm
The Schlossbrücke (Palace Bridge) by Karl Friedrich Schinkel (1821-24), in the background Berlin Cathedral and the television tower

oben: Der Turm der Friedrichswerderschen Kirche zwischen den beiden Kuppeln der St.-Hedwigs-Kathedrale
unten: Das Kaufhaus Galeries Lafayette in der Friedrichstraße

above: The tower of Friedrichswerdersche Church between the twin domes of St Hedwig's Cathedral
below: The Galeries Lafayette department store on Friedrichstrasse

Wohnhaus Sophienstraße, Ecke Große Hamburger Straße

Residential building at the corner of Sophienstrasse and Grosse Hamburger Strasse

Das Restaurant „Refugium" im Französischen Dom am Gendarmenmarkt
The "Refugium" restaurant in the French Cathedral at Gendarmenmarkt

Freitreppe und Säulenhalle des 1818-21 von Karl Friedrich Schinkel erbauten Schauspielhauses, jetzt Konzerthaus Berlin
The Konzerthaus Berlin (1818-21), the concert hall, originally designed as a theatre by Karl Friedrich Schinkel

Am Potsdamer Platz
At Potsdamer Platz

Am Potsdamer Platz, Blick auf das Büro- und Geschäftshaus von Hans Kollhoff
View of the office and commercial building designed by Hans Kollhoff at Potsdamer Platz

Forum des Sony Center am Potsdamer Platz
The Sony Center forum at Potsdamer Platz

Das Weinhaus Huth, das einzige erhaltene Gebäude aus der Vorkriegszeit am Potsdamer Platz
Weinhaus Huth, the only pre-war building that survived at Potsdamer Platz

oben: Reste der Berliner Mauer auf dem Friedhofsgelände an der Bernauer Straße, Mitte
unten: ehemaliger Wachturm der Grenzbefestigung an der Kieler Straße, Mitte

above: Remains of the Berlin Wall at the cemetery on Bernauer Strasse, Mitte
below: One of the old East German border watch-towers on Kieler Strasse, Mitte

Reste der Mauer am Potsdamer Platz
Remains of the Wall at Potsdamer Platz

Kinosaal im Filmpalast am Kurfürstendamm
Inside the Filmpalast cinema on Kurfürstendamm

Schwanenmantel von Marlene Dietrich im Filmmuseum Berlin – Deutsche Kinemathek, Marlene Dietrich Collection, Berlin
Marlene Dietrich's "swan coat" at the Filmmuseum Berlin – Deutsche Kinemathek, Marlene Dietrich Collection, Berlin

Im Diener in der Grolmanstraße, Charlottenburg
Inside Diener's on Grolmanstrasse, Charlottenburg

Im Café Einstein in der Kurfürstenstraße, Tiergarten

In Café Einstein on Kurfürstenstrasse, Tiergarten

Monika Wolff, die Inhaberin von Clärchens Ballhaus in der Auguststraße, Mitte
Monika Wolff, the proprietor of Clärchens Ballhaus on Auguststrasse, Mitte

Michael Würthle und Rainald Nohal, die Inhaber der Paris Bar in Charlottenburg
Michael Würthle and Rainald Nohal, the proprietors of the Paris Bar, Charlottenburg

Im Friedrichstadtpalast
Inside the Friedrichstadtpalast variety theatre

Lutz Deisinger und Holger Klotzbach, die Inhaber der Bar Jeder Vernunft, Wilmersdorf
Lutz Deisinger and Holger Klotzbach, proprietors of the Bar Jeder Vernunft, Wilmersdorf

Die Modedesignerin Claudia Skoda in ihrem Atelier in der Linienstraße, Mitte
The fashion designer, Claudia Skoda, in her studio on Linienstrasse, Mitte

Die Hut-Galerie von Fiona Bennett in der Großen Hamburger Straße, Mitte
Fiona Bennett's hat boutique on Grosse Hamburger Strasse, Mitte

Der Maler Volker Stelzmann in seinem Atelier in der Hochschule der Künste in Charlottenburg
The artist, Volker Stelzmann, in his studio at the Hochschule der Künste, the school of art, in Charlottenburg

Der Schriftsteller Sten Nadolny in der U-Bahn-Station Theodor-Heuss-Platz
The writer, Sten Nadolny, in the metro station at Theodor Heuss Platz

Hinterhof des ehemaligen Wohnhauses von Käthe Kruse in der Fasanenstraße, Charlottenburg
Courtyard of the house in Fasanenstrasse, Charlottenburg, where Käthe Kruse once lived

Das Literaturhaus Berlin in der Fasanenstraße, Charlottenburg
The Literaturhaus Berlin in Fasanenstrasse, Charlottenburg

Schaufenster in der Grolmanstraße in Charlottenburg
Shop window in Grolmanstrasse, Charlottenburg

Im Antiquariat Düwal in der Schlüterstraße, Charlottenburg
Inside Antiquariat Düwal, the rare book shop on Schlüterstrasse, Charlottenburg

Der Artisten- und Varietéhistoriker Markschiess van Trix in seiner Wohnung in Mitte

Markschiess van Trix, historical expert on artistes and variety theatre, in his apartment in Mitte

Otto Ziege, Radsportidol und sportlicher Leiter des Berliner Sechstagerennens

Otto Ziege, cycle racing idol and sport director of the Berlin six-day race

Rundbogenportal mit Atlanten, Eingang zu Riehmers Hofgarten, Kreuzberg
Archway with atlantes at the entrance to Riehmers Hofgarten, Kreuzberg

Ruine des Anhalter Bahnhofs, Kreuzberg
The ruins of Anhalter Bahnhof railway station, Kreuzberg

Wasserturm in der Fidicinstraße, Kreuzberg
Water tower on Fidicinstrasse, Kreuzberg

Ehemalige Kaserne des 1. Garde-Dragoner-Regiments am Mehringdamm in Kreuzberg (1850-53), heute Finanzamt Kreuzberg
The former barracks of the First Dragoon Guards Regiment on Mehringdamm, Kreuzberg (1850-53), now the Kreuzberg inland revenue office

oben: Hinterhof in Prenzlauer Berg
unten: Hinterhof in Friedrichshain

above: A courtyard in Prenzlauer Berg
below: A courtyard in Friedrichshain

Shell-Haus am Reichpietschufer von Emil Fahrenkamp (1930-31), heute Sitz der Hauptverwaltung der BEWAG
The Shell House on Reichpietschufer, designed by Emil Fahrenkamp (1930-31), now the head office of BEWAG, Berlin's electricity service

oben links und oben rechts: Martin-Gropius-Bau, Schmuckreliefs an der Seitenfassade
unten: Martin-Gropius-Bau, Lichthof

above left and right: The Martin Gropius Building, decorative reliefs on the side façade
below: The Martin Gropius Building, the atrium

Das Ischtartor von Babylon im Pergamonmuseum
The Ishtar Gate of Babylon in the Pergamon Museum

In der Gemäldegalerie am Kulturforum
Inside the Picture Gallery at the Kulturforum

Die Haupthalle des Hamburger Bahnhofs (Ausstellung: Das XX. Jahrhundert – Ein Jahrhundert Kunst in Deutschland)
The main hall of the Hamburger Bahnhof (exhibition: The XX Century – a century of art in Germany)

Im Depot des Museums für Naturkunde in Mitte
In the depot of the Natural History Museum in Mitte

Treppenhaus des Museums für Naturkunde
The staircase in the Natural History Museum

Im Depot des Ethnologischen Museums in Dahlem, Masken aus der Südsee (oben), japanische Samurai-Rüstung (unten)

In the depot of the Museum of Ethnology in Dahlem, Masks from the South Seas (above), Japanese Samurai armour (below)

Im Depot des Ethnologischen Museums in Dahlem, Musikinstrumente aus Zaire (oben), Maskengewänder aus Westafrika (unten)

In the depot of the Museum of Ethnology in Dahlem, Musical instruments from Zaire (above), Mask robes from West Africa (below)

Im Depot des Ethnologischen Museums in Dahlem, Abteilung Ostasien
In the depot of the Museum of Ethnology in Dahlem, East Asian section

Im Depot der Antikensammlung im Pergamonmuseum
In the depot of the Antikensammlung, the Greek and Roman collection at the Pergamon Museum

oben: Im ehemaligen Skulpturendepot des Stadtmuseums Berlin im Ephraim-Palais, Mitte
unten: Im Depot des Georg-Kolbe-Museums, Charlottenburg

above: In the former sculpture depot of the Berlin City Museum at the Ephraim Palais, Mitte
below: In the depot of the Georg Kolbe Museum, Charlottenburg

Theatersammlung des Stadtmuseums Berlin in der Schöneberger Straße, Tempelhof,
Puppen von Klaus Noack aus der Inszenierung des Berliner Ensembles von Hanns Eislers „Johann Faustus“

The theatrical collection of the Berlin City Museum in Schöneberger Strasse, Tempelhof; figures by Klaus Noack from the Berliner Ensemble production of Hanns Eisler's "Johann Faustus"

Die Choreographin Sasha Waltz und das Ensemble des Stücks „Körper“ in der Schaubühne am Lehniner Platz
The choreographer, Sasha Waltz, and the ensemble of the production entitled "Körper" (Bodies) at the Schaubühne am Lehniner Platz

Claus Peymann, Intendant des Berliner Ensembles, im Helene-Weigel-Zimmer des Theaters am Bertolt-Brecht-Platz, Mitte
Claus Peymann, the director of the Berliner Ensemble, in the theatre's Helene Weigel room, at Bertolt Brecht Platz in Mitte

Frank Castorf, Intendant der Volksbühne am Rosa-Luxemburg-Platz, Mitte
Frank Castorf, the director of the Volksbühne am Rosa Luxemburg Platz, Mitte

Schaubühne am Lehniner Platz, Wilmersdorf

The Schaubühne am Lehniner Platz, Wilmersdorf

Deutsche Staatsoper Unter den Linden

The German State Opera House on Unter den Linden

oben: Schloß Bellevue in Tiergarten, Amtssitz des Bundespräsidenten
unten: Schloß Tegel, 1820-24 von Karl Friedrich Schinkel umgebaut, ehemals Wohnsitz der Familie Humboldt

above: Bellevue Palace in Tiergarten, the seat of the Federal President
below: Tegel Palace, modernized by Karl Friedrich Schinkel 1820-24, the former home of the Humboldt family

Schloß Charlottenburg, Gartenseite
Charlottenburg Palace seen from the gardens

Der Schinkel-Pavillon (1824-25) im Park des Schlosses Charlottenburg
The Schinkel Pavilion (1824-25) in the park at Charlottenburg Palace

Mausoleum im Park des Schlosses Charlottenburg, Marmorsarkophag mit der Statue der schlafenden Königin Luise von Christian Daniel Rauch (1810-14)

The mausoleum in the park at Charlottenburg Palace, marble sarcophagus with the statue of the sleeping Queen Luise by Christian Daniel Rauch (1810-14)

Treppenhaus im westlichen Kasernenbau der Garde Du Corps von Friedrich August Stüler, Charlottenburg, heute Sitz der Sammlung Berggruen
Staircase in the western barracks block of the Garde du Corps by Friedrich August Stüler, now home of the Berggruen Collection, Charlottenburg

Der Kunstsammler Heinz Berggruen mit Skulpturen von Alberto Giacometti
The art collector, Heinz Berggruen, with sculptures by Alberto Giacometti

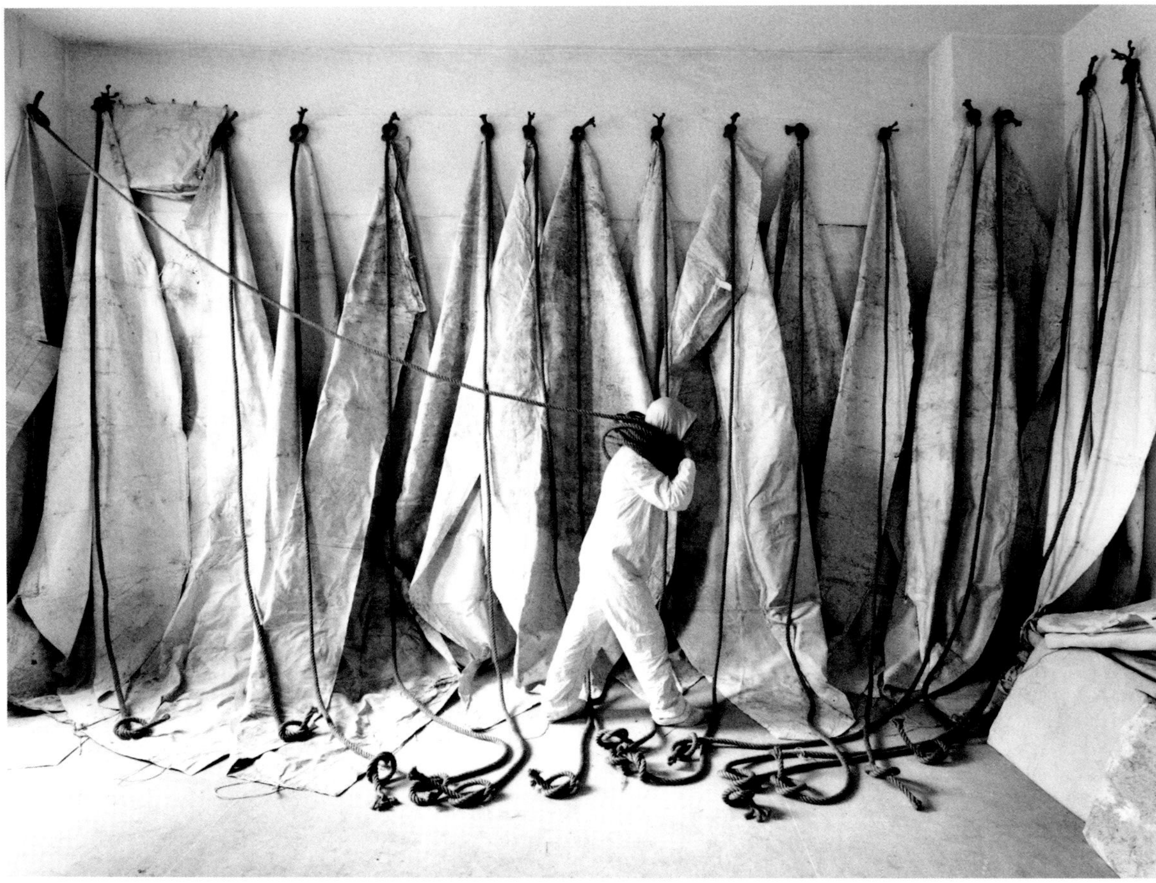

oben: Die koreanische Malerin Ouhi Cha bei ihrer Performance „A Ship of Odyssey“ in ihrer Wohnung in Wilmersdorf
unten: Der Maler Max Neumann in seinem Kreuzberger Atelier

above: The Korean artist, Ouhi Cha, during her performance "A Ship of Odyssey" in her apartment in Wilmersdorf
below: The artist, Max Neumann, in his Kreuzberg studio

Im Atelier des Malers und Bildhauers Rainer Fetting in Kreuzberg
In the studio of the artist, Rainer Fetting, in Kreuzberg

Der Bildgießer Hermann Noack vor einer Plastik von Rainer Kriester
Hermann Noack, the metal casting expert, in front of a work by Rainer Kriester

Der Aktionskünstler Ben Wargin
The action artist, Ben Wargin

Der Galerist Florian Karsch in der Galerie Nierendorf, Charlottenburg
The gallery owner, Florian Karsch, in the Galerie Nierendorf, Charlottenburg

Der Maler Thomas Hartmann in seinem Kreuzberger Atelier
The artist, Thomas Hartmann, in his studio in Kreuzberg

Die 1842 von A. Borsig gebaute Lokomotive „Beuth“, Deutsches Technikmuseum Berlin, Kreuzberg
The “Beuth” engine built in 1842 by A. Borsig, at the German Museum of Technology Berlin in Kreuzberg

Im AEG-Archiv, Deutsches Technikmuseum Berlin, Kreuzberg
In the AEG archive at the German Museum of Technology Berlin in Kreuzberg

Innenhöfe in der Oberbaum-City in Friedrichshain
Courtyards in the Oberbaum-City in Friedrichshain

Ehemalige Goerzwerke in der Rheinstraße, Steglitz
The former Goerzwerke in Rheinstrasse, Steglitz

Treppenhaus im Rundfunkzentrum Köpenick in der Nalepastraße
Staircase in the Broadcasting Centre Köpenick in Nalepastrasse

Aufgang zur Lithographie-Anstalt Meisenbach und Riffarth, Schöneberg
Entrance to the printing firm Meisenbach und Riffarth, Schöneberg

oben: Parfümeriefabrik Schwarzkopf in Tempelhof (1928-30)
unten: Gelände der ehemaligen Versuchsanstalt für Luftfahrt, Adlershof

above: The Schwarzkopf perfume factory in Tempelhof (1928-30)
below: At the former aeronautical test grounds in Adlershof

oben: Ullsteinhaus in Tempelhof (1925-26)
unten: Umspannwerk Wilhelmsruh in Pankow (1925-26)

above: Ullsteinhaus in Tempelhof (1925-26)
below: Wilhelmsruh transformer station in Pankow (1925-26)

Funkturm auf dem Messegelände Berlin, erbaut 1924-26, und Messehalle aus dem Jahr 1936
The Funkturm transmission tower built 1924-26 on the exhibition grounds, and a hall built in 1936

Blick vom Turm des Rathauses Spandau auf den neuen Bahnhof Berlin-Spandau
View of the new Berlin-Spandau railway station from the tower of Spandau Town Hall

Blick auf die S-Bahn-Strecke Richtung Potsdam mit dem S-Bahnhof Savignyplatz
View of the line to Potsdam at Savignyplatz S-Bahn station

S-Bahnhof Mexikoplatz, Zehlendorf
Mexikoplatz S-Bahn station, Zehlendorf

S-Bahnhof Nikolassee, Zehlendorf
Nikolassee S-Bahn station, Zehlendorf

oben: Wohnhaus Ahornallee 47, erbaut 1870-71 von dem Schinkel-Schüler Eduard Titz
unten: Villa Harteneck in Wilmersdorf, erbaut 1911 von Adolf Wollenberg

above: Residential building at Ahornallee 47, built 1870-71 to designs by the Schinkel pupil Eduard Titz
below: Villa Harteneck in Wilmersdorf, built 1911 to designs by Adolf Wollenberg

oben: Wohn- und Atelierhaus Dr. Walter Menne, Spandau-Kladow, 1964-66 erbaut von Werner Düttmann
unten: Haus Baensch in Berlin-Gatow, erbaut 1934-35 von Hans Scharoun

above: Residential and studio building of Dr Walter Menne in Spandau-Kladow 1964-66, designed by Werner Düttmann
below: Haus Baensch in Berlin-Gatow 1934-35, designed by Hans Scharoun

Nazarethkirche am Leopoldplatz in Wedding, 1832-35 erbaut von Karl Friedrich Schinkel
The Nazareth Church at Leopoldplatz in Wedding 1832-35, designed by Karl Friedrich Schinkel

Dorfkirche Stolpe am Wilhelmplatz in Berlin-Wannsee, 1858-59 erbaut von Friedrich August Stüler

Stolpe village church at Wilhelmplatz in Berlin-Wannsee, built 1858-59 to designs by Friedrich August Stüler

Dorotheenstädtischer Friedhof, Mitte. Grabmale Georg Wilhelm Friedrich Hegels (oben), Helene Weigels und Bertolt Brechts (unten)

Dorotheenstadt Cemetery, Mitte. The graves of Georg Wilhelm Friedrich Hegel (above) and of Helene Weigel and Bertolt Brecht (below)

Südwest-Friedhof Stahnsdorf. Grabmale Heinrich Zilles (oben) und Friedrich Wilhelm Murnaus (unten)

Südwest Cemetery Stahnsdorf. The graves of Heinrich Zille (above) and of Friedrich Wilhelm Murnau (below)

Jüdischer Friedhof Weißensee
The Jewish cemetery in Weissensee

Blick auf die Glienicker Brücke aus der „Großen Neugierde" von Karl Friedrich Schinkel (1835) im Park Klein-Glienicke
View of Glienicke bridge from panorama viewing tower designed by Karl Friedrich Schinkel (1835) in Klein Glienicke park

Park Klein-Glienicke, Stibadium von Ludwig Persius (1840)
Garden seat in Klein Glienicke park designed by Ludwig Persius (1840)

Pfaueninsel, Kavaliershaus, 1824-26 erbaut von Karl Friedrich Schinkel
The Cavalier House on Peacock Island, built 1824-26 to designs by Karl Friedrich Schinkel

Pfaueninsel, Blick auf das Schloß, 1794-97 erbaut von Johann Gottlieb Brendel
View of the palace on Peacock Island, built 1794-97 to designs by Johann Gottlieb Brendel

MANFRED HAMM

geboren 1944 in Zwickau, gehört zu den Altmeistern der Berlin-Photographie. Mit Buchveröffentlichungen und Ausstellungen im In- und Ausland hat er sich insbesondere als Architektur- und Industriephotograph einen Namen gemacht. Mit seinen Arbeiten ist er in zahlreichen internationalen Sammlungen und Museen vertreten.
Manfred Hamm lebt und arbeitet in Berlin.

KLAUS HARTUNG

geboren 1940 in Olbernhau/Erzgebirge, ist einer der besten Kenner Berlins und seiner Geschichte.
Seit 1992 ist er Berliner Korrespondent der ZEIT.
Er hat zahlreiche Essays, Artikel und Features sowie die Bücher „Die neuen Kleider der Psychiatrie" (1980) und „Neunzehnhundertneunundachtzig" (1990) veröffentlicht.
Klaus Hartung lebt in Berlin.

MANFRED HAMM

was born in 1944 in Zwickau and is an established figure in the Berlin photographic scene. His reputation is based in particular on his architectural and industrial photography, and he has published books and held exhibitions both in Germany and abroad. His work can be found in numerous international collections and museums.
Manfred Hamm lives and works in Berlin.

KLAUS HARTUNG

was born in Olbernhau/Erzgebirge in 1940 and is among the leading experts on Berlin and its history. Since 1992, he has been the Berlin correspondent for "Die Zeit". He has published numerous essays, articles and features as well as the books "Die neuen Kleider der Psychiatrie" (1980) and "Neunzehnhundertneunundachtzig" (1990).
Klaus Hartung lives in Berlin.

Von diesem Buch ist eine Vorzugsausgabe mit einer signierten und numerierten Originalphotographie in einer Auflage von 350 Exemplaren erschienen.

This book has also been published in a limited special edition of 350 copies, which include a signed and numbered original photograph.

Abdruck der Schwarzpläne mit freundlicher Genehmigung der Senatsverwaltung für Stadtentwicklung Berlin.

Übersetzung: Joseph O'Donnell (Essay),
Ann Robertson (Bildunterschriften)
Lektorat: Diethelm Kaiser, Berlin
Gestaltung: Dorén + Köster, Berlin
Lithographie: NovaConcept, Berlin
Druck: H. Heenemann, Berlin
Bindung: Lüderitz & Bauer, Berlin

Umschlagmotiv: Kuppel des Reichstags

Printed in Germany

ISBN 3-87584-859-4